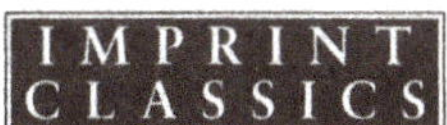

Margaret Preston in Berowra

An exploration of the influence of place on her art and craft practice

Rhonda Davis

ETT IMPRINT
Exile Bay

This Imprint Classics edition published in 2025.

First published by ETT Imprint, Exile Bay June 2021
Second revised edition published December 2021

ETT IMPRINT
PO Box R1906
Royal Exchange NSW 1225
Australia

ISBN 978-1-922473-87-1 (paper)
ISBN 978-1-922473-32-5 (ebook)

Cover photograph of Margret Preston at home in her garden in Berowra by Frederick Halmarick, 1937

Cover, edit and internal design by Tom Thompson

The publisher is grateful to the Trustee of the Estate Late Margaret Preston the Permanent Trustee Limited, for permissions to reproduce the images and writings of Margaret Preston in all our editions for Mark

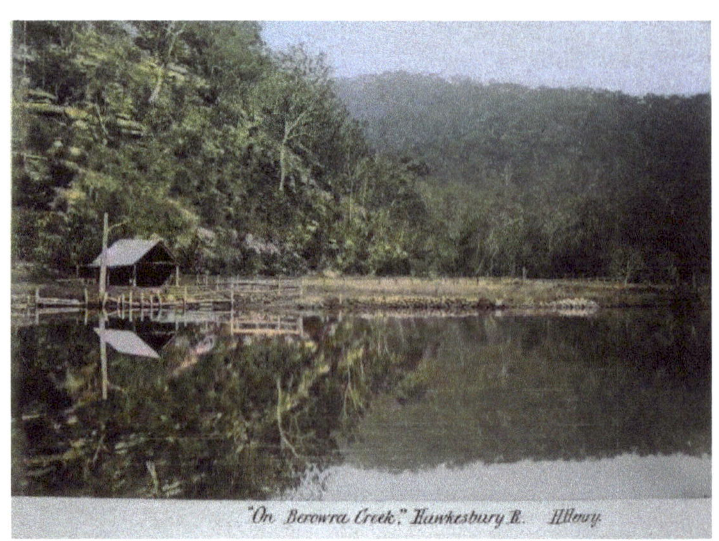

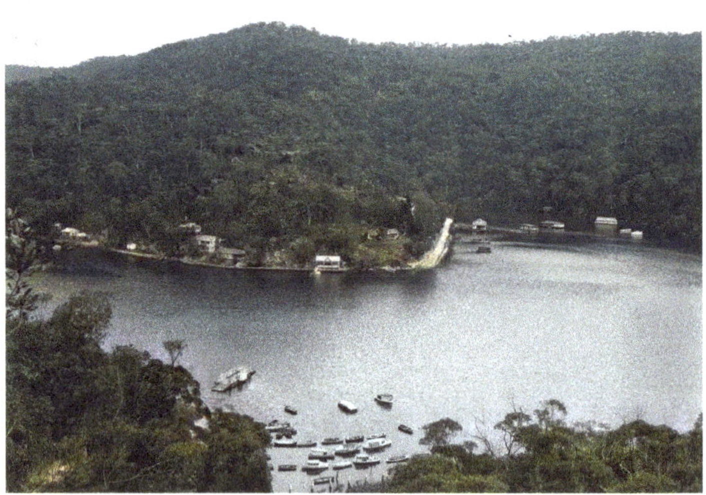

Berowra Creek, 1925.
Berowra Waters 1932.

Contents

Introduction

Berowra has long been, and continues to be, a close-knit community, with local knowledge transmitted from one generation to the next. It weaves the fabric of a bushland community steeped within the history of place and people. I first came to Berowra in 1982 and it was here that I met my future husband, Mark Davis.

Mark grew up in Berowra, where he spent much of his youth in the bush exploring the many facets that make up this unique landscape. Berowra Waters became his main stomping ground for himself and his friends – they camped most weekends. At every step, Mark knew the bush intimately and was later to introduce me to those experiential facets. We succumbed to the brilliance of the colours, formations, textures, and scents of the sandstone, the rocks, the rock holes, the caves, and the native bushes on our many excursions over a three-decade period.

The pervasiveness of those intergenerational connections is evident in the way Mark's Aunty Elaine, nee Davis, was married to Bill Foster who was the grocery boy for Margaret Preston and had direct contact with her.

The penultimate of arriving at a metaphysical perception that presence and absence pervades historical investigation is to imagine the beginning as the end and vice versa. To this, the plausibility of retracing the life of artist Margaret Preston in Berowra was to consolidate my own deeply felt connections with this special place, an ongoing investigation enshrined within the memories of my late husband.

Berowra

Berowra, Aboriginal word berara, translates as 'a place of many winds', and as 'shells'. The deep layers of middens embedded along Berowra Creek provide a direct link with the past; reimagining the activities of the Traditional Custodians of the land, magnifying the importance of this landscape. The middens remain robust and undisturbed in providing tangible evidence to the long history of and continued occupation of the Dharug and Guringai peoples of this area.[1]

In 1928, Margaret Preston underwent major surgery, reputedly a consequence of breast cancer. In a letter dated 27 July of the same year, Preston wrote to her art dealer, Basil Burdett, from a private hospital bed at The Terraces, Paddington. It appears she was suffering from a life-threatening illness but does not hesitate to curse the art critic, G. Shaw, in a somewhat caustic manner:

'This is a faint note … as soon as I get over the weakness by my "chopping" I like Miss Proctor and will write [to] her as soon as the new maid can bring in Tea properly – … I'm really out to kill Shaw [G. Shaw] – you see my peep "over the edge" hasn't Christianised me a bit Im still after his Gore – will be home in a week or two.'

Presumably, Preston endured the pain and trauma of a mastectomy, as the reference to 'chopping' alludes to an external surgical intervention. The gravity of her condition would have been major concern for both Preston and her husband, William. No doubt, Preston's dire need for rest and recuperation informed their decision to move to Berowra, escaping the bustle of city life to this quiet rural hideaway.

Berowra has a fairly high altitude, similar to parts of the Blue Mountains, and in the early part of the 20th century it was promoted as an optimum environment for those suffering ill health. People flocked to

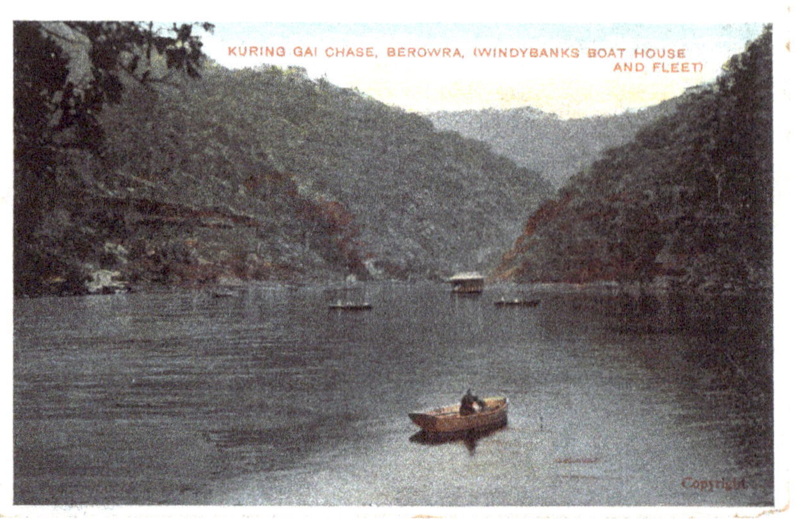

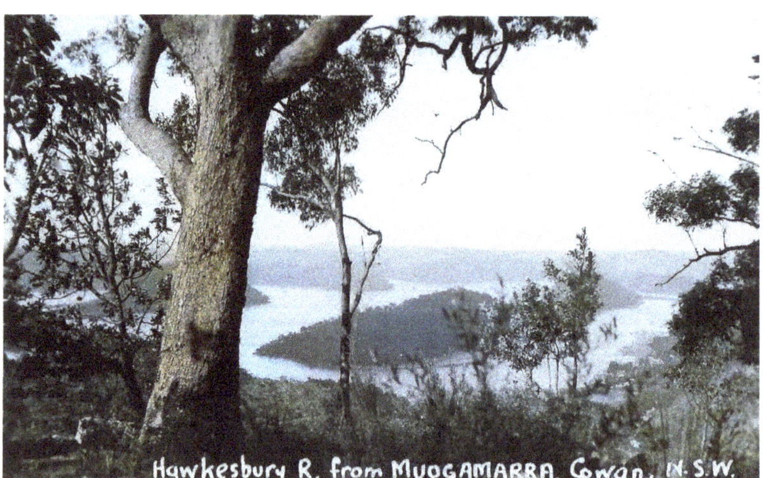

Windybanks Boathouse 1925.
The view from Cowan, 1932.

this area on weekends. The real estate agent, Arthur Rickard & Co. Ltd, wrote a testimonial to this effect in the brochure titled 'Beautiful Berowra':

'To those of us who live by the shore, or close to sea level, the air of Berowra is a real tonic, stimulating, but without aftereffects. Even in your weekends spent there, you will be able to store up enough energy and vitality to brace the whole week. Making your home there would be guaranteeing for yourself and your family that greatest of all blessings – perfect health.'[2]

Preston's move to Berowra paralleled a new movement of botanical interest in native plants and identifying what plants were indigenous to specific areas. The veracity of studying native flowers close up in their natural habitat allowed Preston for the first time to absorb and understand aspects of plant ecology. The combined aesthetics of art and science became the core of her practice during the Berowra period. Preston lost interest in what she referred to as 'garden ones' and concentrated more on native flowers unfolding to seasonal changes. She provides this insight into her new way of working in a letter she writes to her art dealer, John Young: '[I] Should be [able to] start work in Aug – as all the flowers will be out then'.[3] By November, Preston had sent Young a new set of woodblock prints depicting the native plants on her property: 'I am so pleased – many thanks about fresh work ... The native flowers are passing and I am not interested in garden ones'.[4]

At Berowra, Preston was able to understand native flowers in relation to the natural environment, fundamental to her binding the canvas with an amalgam of ideas and new ways of working. Her new surrounds extended her perceptual view of relational size contrasted to the imposed, constructed geometry and scale of traditional still life arrangements she had been pursuing. Preston's mode of production changed too. No longer at the mercy of flower growers; instead, she could step into her own backyard and encounter native flowers in the wild, at any pace and at any time of day or night.

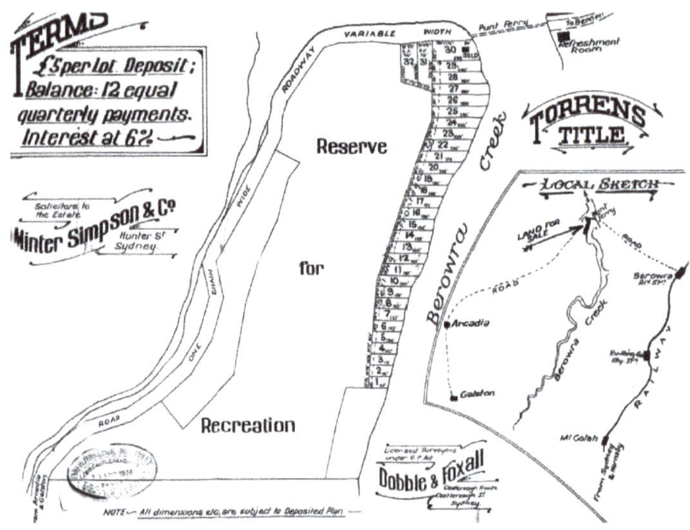

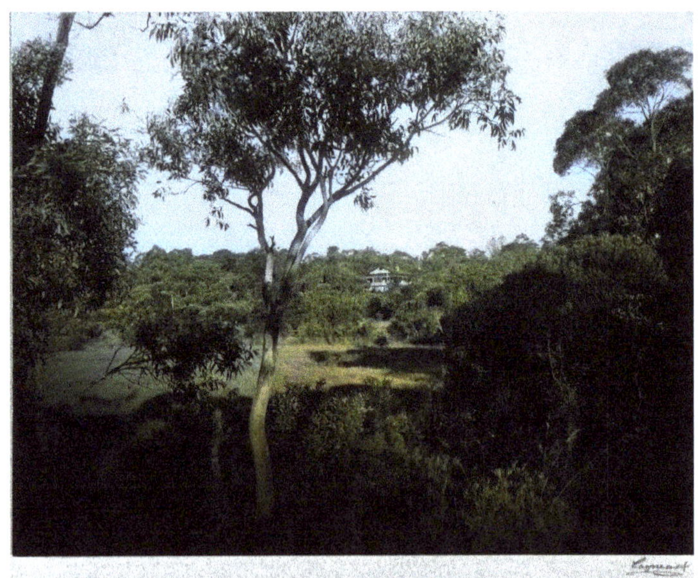

The first sale of town lots in Berowra, 1926.
Distant view of Margaret Preston's house at Berowra
by Harold Cazneaux, 1936.

'The Springs' Property

On 21 August 1931, lot 60, Stewart Street, Berowra, transferred to William Preston, named as Company Director, and his wife, Margaret Rose Preston. The property consisted of 8 acres, 2 roods and 17 perches (3.48 hectares) and cost 200 pounds. In the following year, on 29 March 1932, legal title to lot 59, which contained a watercourse, also transferred to the Prestons. This extra acquisition created a much larger property than previous writings have revealed. To be exact, on 11 April 1932, the property comprised 11 acres and 17 perches – an area of about 4.5 hectares.

This information lends new insights into the way the Prestons searched for property as early as 1931 and what was to become the only home they ever purchased. The property was known as 'The Springs' and described by locals as the showpiece of the area. It is recorded in 1916 that a Mr and Mrs Willoughby Devlin threw a 'house party' inviting guests to celebrate the naming of their new home in Berowra called 'The Springs'.[5] By 1926, a Mr G.K. Freeman and his wife lived at The Springs.[6] The last occupiers prior to the Prestons' purchase of Lot 60 were John Knorr Aulsebrook and Leycester Hudson Greaves, both listed as farmers. Curiously, William Preston did retain the lease on their previous house at 11 Park Avenue, Mosman, until 1956, which suggests the couple used it as a base camp when they visited the city.

In contrast to the Federation homes built in the Berowra area, the architectural refurbishment of the Prestons' house was innovative for its time. Unusually striking was the low-pitched roof. Preston merged the stylistic developments of the Californian bungalow with aspects borrowed from the Arts and Crafts Movement in creating the epitome of the modern home.

She used the concept of 'design for living' as the impetus for undertaking major renovations to the existing house. Finding the rooms to be small and confined, she arranged to have walls knocked down in the hallway. 'One side of the hall was removed from the door leading into the living room down to the end of that room…She thus gained the width of the hall in vista without losing her entrance increasing the effect of space without actually sacrificing anything.'[7] The walls washed in pastel shades effectively opened up the living room generating more light within the space. At the entrance of the living room, Preston made a low settee that continued around to the fireplace in an L-shaped arrangement. This handcrafted piece of furniture, meticulously upholstered in a streamlined fashion – flat, angular – was uncomplicatedly striking. Preston made cushions from what was called Durex Art felt, which came in 35 different shades.[8] Using a range of contrasting and vivid colours, arranged impeccably on the settee, expressed the tangibility of the material creating comfort and warmth in winter.

The floors, covered in inexpensive matting, possibly sourced from Anthony Hordern & Sons store, since her husband was the company director, created an original, modern look. Anthony Hordern & Sons publicised its available matting floor coverings that certainly matched Preston's aesthetic taste: 'The patterns and colourings are distinctly Oriental, bold geometrical designs being woven in Browns, Blues, Greens, and Reds.'[9] The space permeated with a modernism borne out of the decorative arts, it was a house, a home, and all-encompassing to the senses.

Preston, satisfied with the completion of the renovations, allowed *The Australian Home Beautiful* to feature the house and property in the magazine, superbly captured by acclaimed photographer, Harold Cazneaux.[10] Preston was not visible in these photographs, but they conveyed her presence as tastemaker of the modern home. Cazneaux undertook the majority of the shoot in 1936 and completed the assignment in the summer period of the following year. The images revealed the interior of the Prestons' living room with the beam of the mid-morning sun from the north-east hitting the wall of the fireplace and corner settee. The space encompasses a stark beauty and stillness, void of activity.

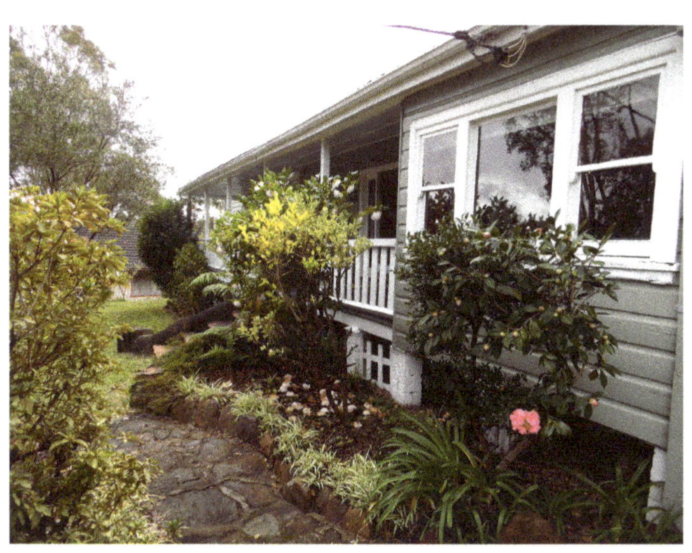

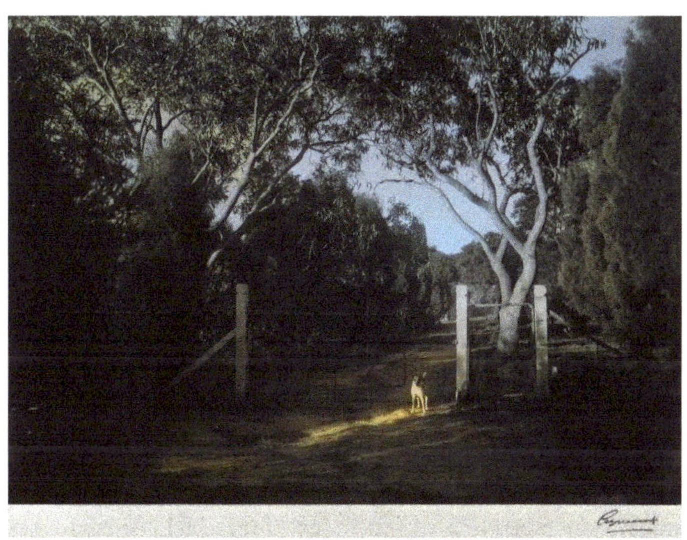

'The Springs', as it stands now.
Entrance to the driveway, by Harold Cazneaux, 1936.

The following year, Fairfax photographer FJ Halmarick photographed Preston within the home, revealing her everyday spaces. We enter the living room with Preston sitting at ease, turning the pages of a large book resting on her lap. Glimpsed from underneath, the book is titled *Art of the US*. The scene evokes a palpable and quiet determination of a cosmopolitan and modern woman relaxed within the comfort of her country home. Surrounded by an array of artworks, objects, books, rugs and materials, with some collected on her many overseas travels, Preston appears attuned to her immediate surroundings. Evidently, the magnificent painting, *Implement blue*, which she created in 1927, travelled with her from Mosman to the Berowra home. It is shown alongside what can be identified as one of Thea Proctor's fan paintings. In comparison to Cazneaux's images taken a few months before, this photograph shows an extra picture on the wall placed next to the window. It is an unattributed drawing of a waterfall scene, perhaps illustrating *Blue Pools* at Devlins Creek. The library houses a variety of art books, neatly stacked, with an oriental vase placed on top of the bookshelf. The decorative vase filled with a spectacular arrangement of local Australian rock lilies, once growing profusely in rock shelters throughout the Berowra bushland, parades Preston's affiliation with local native flowers. Preston appears pensive seated under an art deco lamp, which is connected by a running cord to electricity. The scene preserves a charm and beauty of immaculate order.

Plain holland linen curtains diffused the room with a radiant light, where basking in the late afternoon sunlight on the low settee would have been inviting. Cleared of ash and debris left over from the winter months, the fireplace displayed a large kava bowl the Prestons may have collected on their trip to Tahiti and the Pacific Islands in 1933. A maze of objects adorned the shelves above the fireplace – expressions of Preston's interest in and affiliation with Eastern cultures. The shrunken head positioned at the top middle of the fireplace betrays her fascination for the bizarre and associated curio trade, which witnessed the illegal and disturbing trafficking of shrunken heads. However, during this period, the Ecuadorian and Peruvian governments outlawed this practice so Westerners could no longer exploit this unethical and disrespectful form of collecting.

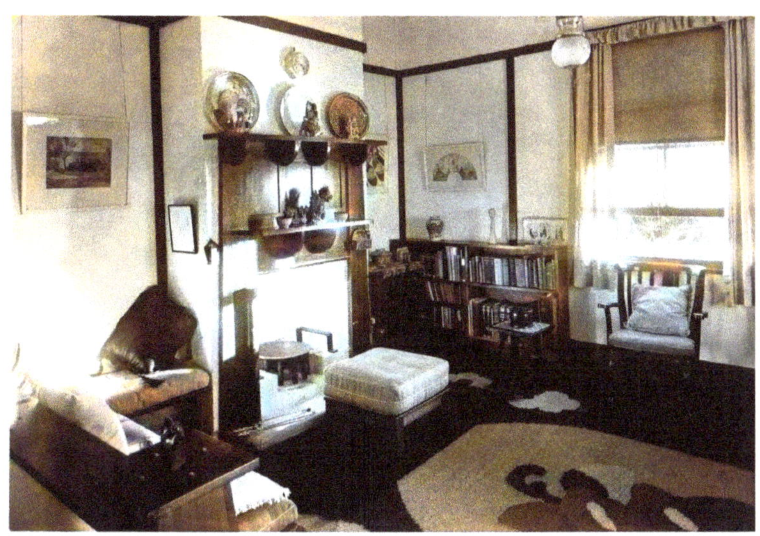

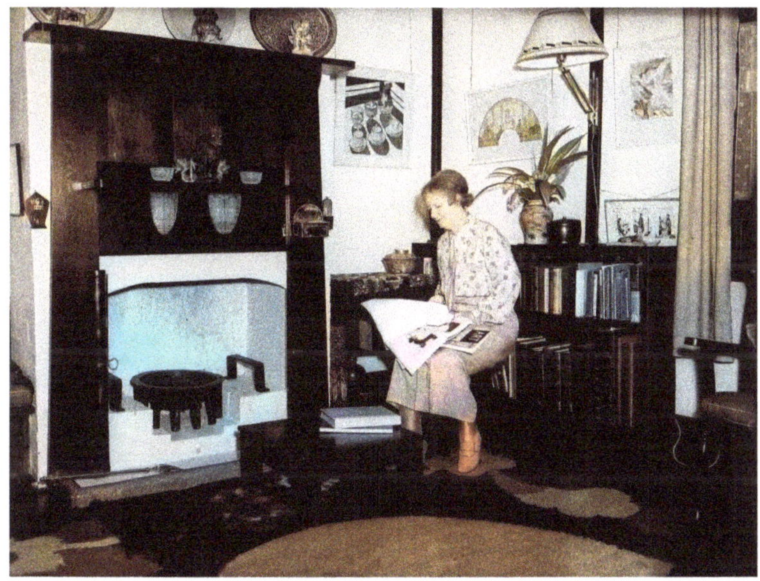

Margaret Preston's living room, Berowra by Harold Cazneaux, 1937.
Preston in the living room by Frederick Halmarick, 1937.

Home / Place

The Prestons' country home, a place that nestled on the 'plains' and looked across 'deep blue-shaded gullies', was filled with the prosperity of their lives. To keep her 'outlook refreshed' Preston embarked on regular annual trips overseas with her husband while living in Berowra. Acutely aware of the influence the Berowra home had on her practice, she always relished the return to home: 'I have feeling for the bush … I never do any sketching when I'm away from home … I like to live with my subjects. I have the feeling of this bush up here and I never use a studio. I paint all over the place, out on the verandah, under the trees, anywhere the spirit moves me.'[11]

The natural growth of the expansive native gardens created an overall aromatic visual display throughout the property. The more structured growth of waratahs and native roses close by the front doorsteps of the house took Preston to work more outdoors. No longer confined within the walls of a studio space, Preston's inexorable energy cleaved a bush aesthetic that ultimately redirected her art production. An extension made to the verandah provided Preston a comfortable concession if the weather prevented her from working outside. William Preston occupied an office space that ran off the verandah adjacent to the right of the front door. Essentially, the couple worked on the same ground at opposite ends.

It was a home; subject to everyday activities and daily rituals that revolve around living spaces. The Preston household, though, was different, in that the couple could afford hired help, which enabled Preston more focused time for pursuing a range of artistic endeavours. Entranced by the comforts home ownership brings, she spent much of her time at the Berowra property. 'If you ever want to see me just come up here – I'm always home and one can talk in comfort in one's own surroundings,' she wrote to her art dealer, John Young.[12]

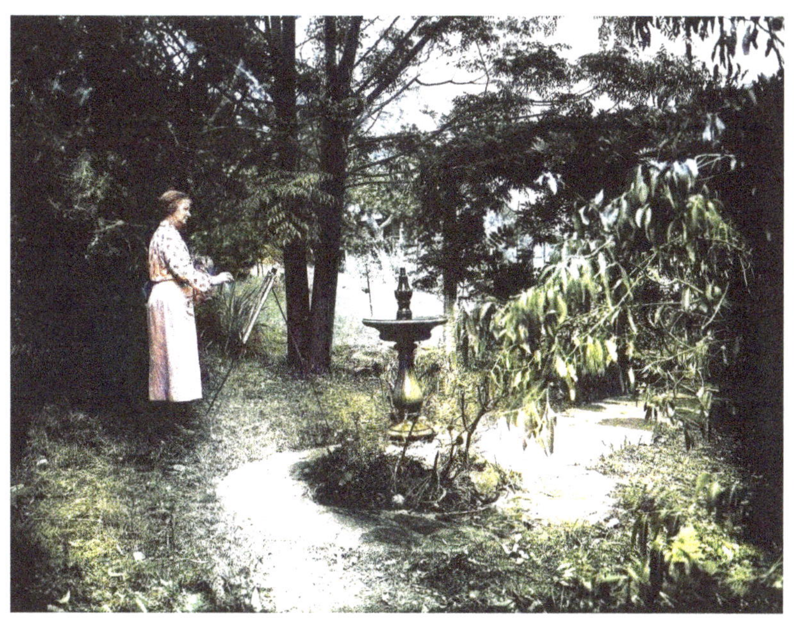

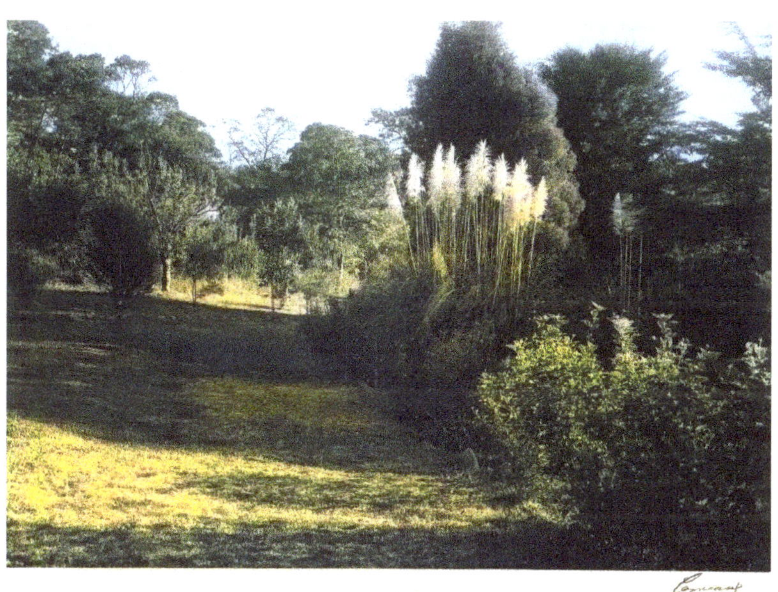

Margret Preston at home in her garden, by Frederick Halmarick, 1937.
Margaret Preston's garden, by Harold Cazneaux, 1936.

Garden and Surrounds

The Springs property contained an oval-shaped natural water reserve that extended at the lower north-west end of the house. The reservoir spanned a large area of about 24 x 18 feet (5.5 x 7.3 meters) and provided a plentiful stream of clean running water. Its perimeter was enclosed by willows, bulrushes and other water grasses keeping the property cool in the summer months.

The Prestons worked arduously together in the garden. Margaret wore a 'wide-brimmed garden hat set firmly over her hair which will obstinately curl she is out and about the garden at all hours and in all weathers, supervising its welfare with that capable practical enthusiasm which she brings to everything she does.'[13] Working together, the Prestons created an ornamental, Japanese-inspired bridge leading to the spring: 'the concrete bridge over the creek has been carried out by Mr Preston himself, with his wife's able assistance, for her creative faculty, like that of many another artist does not by any means confine itself to making pictures'.[14] The springs and its overflow acquired the name of Devlins Creek.

Bill Foster, once a local resident and the Prestons' former grocery deliverer, recalled:

'The Warrina Street Oval was once a natural spring, which contained a big well. It was known as Devlins Creek. Huge rock clearances nestled the rock pools to give a lovely swimmer. There was always water running through with an entrance bridge, you could cross that creek on the bush track that leads further down the valley.'

Even though there is no physical evidence of the bridge remaining, one can imagine the bridge was built as an access pathway that would lead the Prestons to a magnificent Aboriginal rock engraving site. Modern-day drains and pipes have concealed the waterfall and introduced vegetation has overgrown the aquatic site and the Aboriginal rock engravings. Small rock pools and the sound of trickling water offer fragments of the site's former character. The woodblock print titled *The Blue Pool, Berowra*, circa 1933, has never been located nor do we have any evidence of its visual characteristics. Nevertheless, the work's edition sold well in Melbourne at Sedon Galleries. In response to her dealer's demand for more samples of this print, Preston replied, 'Yes - I will send you more "Pools" – either this week or next – also a new block'.[15] If *The Blue Pool, Berowra* were to one day resurface it would provide a key insight into Preston's methodologies of drawing upon reality. An artwork of immense local and national significance.

The property comprised a mix of cultivated land harvesting a bountiful supply of citrus fruits, an English-style garden with 250 varieties of roses, and a wide variety of native plants. The mixed orchard was located on the south side of the house and produced some of the best oranges in the district. 'Hundreds of cases of the finest oranges and lemons are shipped in season from Berowra'.[16] Invariably, Preston's kitchen cupboards filled with the finest of bottled fruit and homemade jams delectably sourced from an ongoing supply from the fruit trees that grew on the property.

The evenly spaced plantation of nut pines that lined the driveway acted as a screen barrier against the harsh and biting south-easterly winds that swept up from the ocean across the valley. The introduced species of coral trees, pines and willows traversed the property in striking contrast to the native bushland. A mechanical pump irrigated the entire property from the natural springs.[17] Along the property's eastern horizon, cattle grazed on the steep hills of the adjacent acreage known as Nicholls Dairy. Extending down behind the Prestons' fowl runs, coral trees screened the properties from each other. Nicholls Dairy today is Berowra Public School. The surviving coral trees, located behind the school, continue to provide a vibrant flowering display during the winter months as they did in the 1930s.

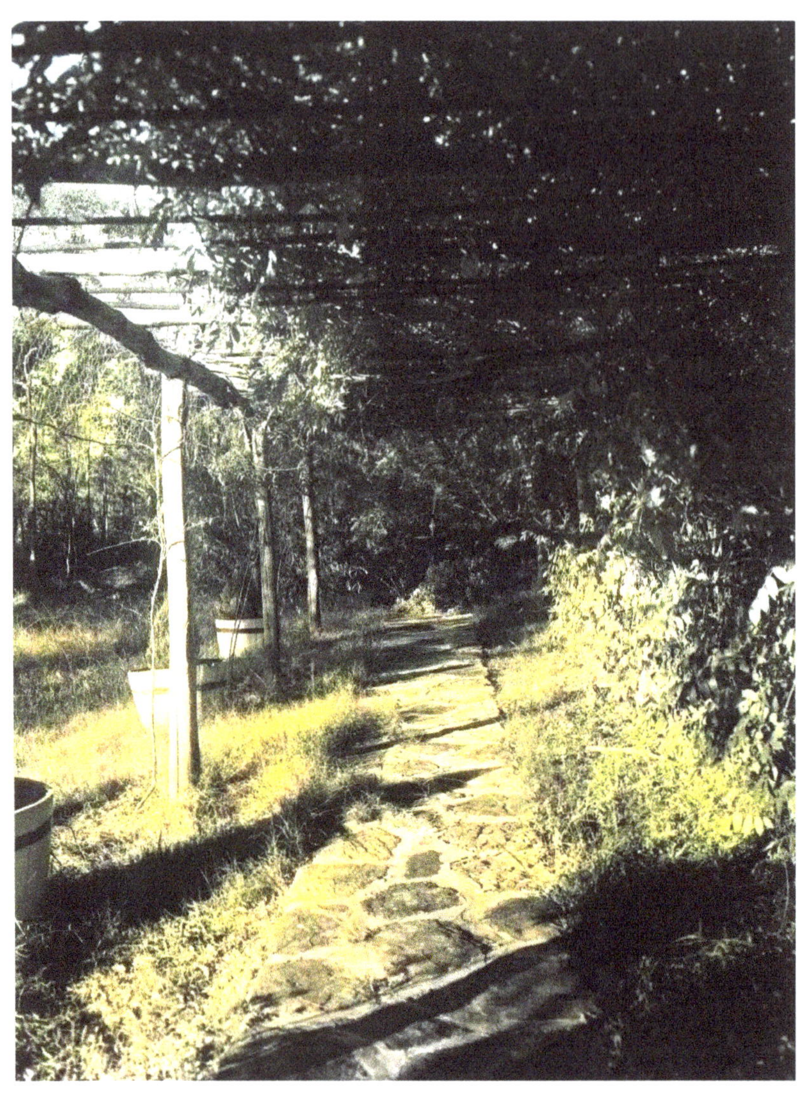

Stone walkway (pergola at Margaret Preston's house, Berowra) by Harold Cazneaux, 1936.

North of the property stood scribbly gum country and by the photographic essays taken of Preston in her surrounds one can ascertain a fire trail running vertically on top of the ridge. Preston gravitated towards the quiet spaces and could be found whiling away an hour or two in the presence of an old gnarly banksia, which affirmed and nourished her spiritual life. She portrayed this banksia in a colour monoprint as a powerful aberration with branches entangled soaring towards a clear night sky. The work is unforgettable.

'But of all the trees in her garden the one that Margaret Preston perhaps loves best of all is an old Banksia tree away down in one of the remotest corners of her domain ... it has been the source of much inspiration and understanding ... To Margaret Preston there is a life time of study in just one old tree, and there is nothing she loves better than to indulge in a contemplative mood for an hour or two in its company.'[18]

Visitors to The Springs could have easily missed the entrance, which was somewhat hidden and 500 metres from the dirt road that was once Stewart Street (now Hillcrest Road). Guests were greeted at the gate by two 'exuberant' and much-adored fox terriers, Kim and Digger before proceeding along the driveway, which formed a gentle slope uphill towards the house. 'Its feeling of seclusion is intensified by the smoothy turfed entrance drive which drowns all sound of approaching wheels. It makes a fitting approach to a garden in which for once our lovely Australian flora is accorded the place of honor.'[19] Edged on either side of the driveway grew the torch plant, native plum, and the pink and red varieties of bottlebrush, punctuated by the more architectural form of the blue eucalyptus. A verdant growth of native cypress trees made an impressive entrance for visitors who frequented the property on weekends.

The Ure Smiths were frequent visitors to The Springs. Sam, the eldest son, from his childhood memories recalled spending lengths of time during the holidays with the Prestons at Berowra:

'She [Preston] loved children and gave beautiful children's parties at Berowra with all kinds of games and competitions. There were usually about a dozen or so children, and the Ure Smiths were usually there … Old Worlde quite sophisticated in character with games like croquet and Pin-the-tail on the Donkey.'[20]

The idea to serve jellies at these parties the Prestons hosted came from their neighbour, Mrs Nicholls. Locals recall the array of bright-coloured jellies Mrs Nicholls would lay out on the tables outside for the children to devour. The Prestons relished the ritual of serving tea on the property's 'terraced lawn' in front of the house shaded by jacarandas. On one of these occasions, guests included cultural and medical luminaries. Among them were Miss Florence Sulman, an artist and one of the daughters of Sir John Sulman ; Professor Victor Bailey , a well-known and inspiring physicist; and Dr Violet Plummer and Miss Eleanor Plummer from Adelaide.[21]

Margaret Preston pottered around the meandering garden and surrounding bushland, a daily routine for working through ideas. The pergola that stretched across the side of the house facing north featured a magnificent flagstone pathway. In its construction, Hawkesbury opal-tinted sandstone locally sourced from the rich deposits on top of the ridge to the eastern side of the house made an opulent display. (Its present-day location is Huntingdon Place.) The pergola covered in climbing roses with juniper trees growing in old washtubs gleaned an enticing space. Reaching the end of the pergola came a circular pathway which led through an unmanicured garden with a modern-style fountain featured in the middle. The fountain appeared to be constructed of a sandstone base with a single tier. On rare occasions, as captured by Cazneaux in his 1936 photograph, the fountain threw a magnificent surge of water in its tranquil setting. Indeed, water was precious given a severe water shortage during the mid 1930s that rationed every household as the tanks got low to two buckets of water each day.

In response to the rationing of water, the Prestons arranged the construction of a well in the far end at the back of the house. Preston

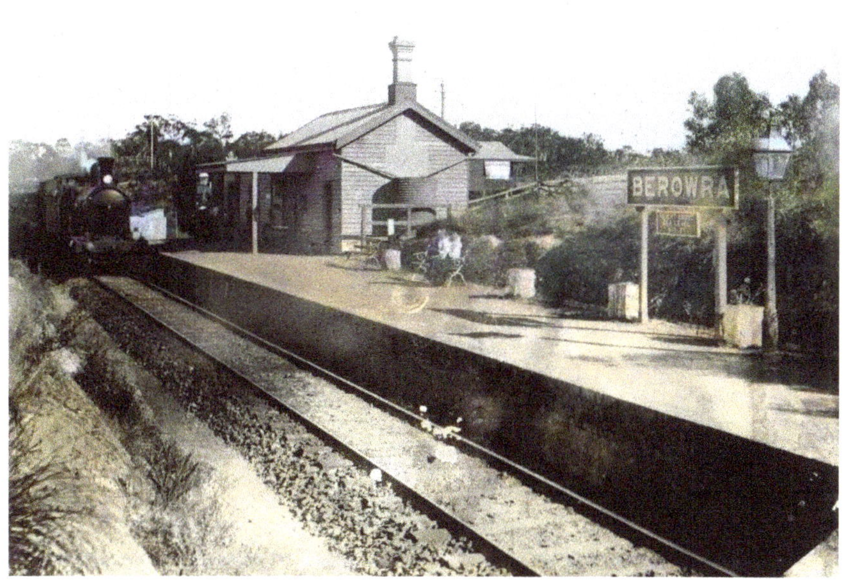

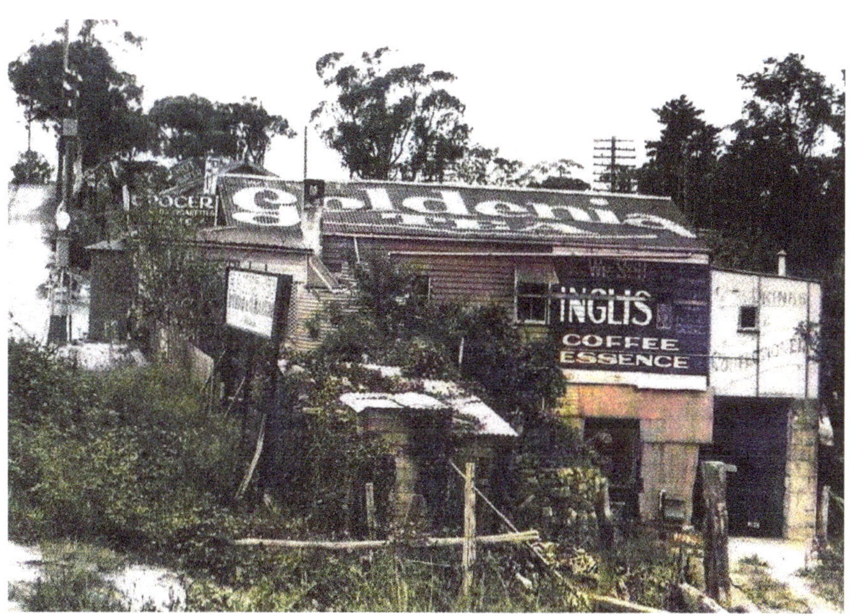

Berowra Station (top) and Foster's Store, Berowra, 1935.

modelled the woodblock print, *The fountain,* 1932, on the real fountain from her garden depicted in a symbolist fashion. The curvilinear forms that undulate in a rhythmic pattern whereby the fountain, garden, gum trees and blue-sky interlock to an incandescent glow, simulates an intensely time presence. Continuing to be inspired by her surrounds, Preston illustrated a newly built garage on the property, which housed their prized tanned/grey-coloured Oldsmobile, in the woodblock print, *The garage*. The work stylised with its red roof and nearby tall gum trees is somewhat enigmatic like *The fountain* in relation to time and space. The artwork shows the rear view of the garage as it slopes towards the north-west and according to the rates notice the garage was built between 1933 and 1935 . These prints essentially qualify Prestons' surrounds as a renewed source of energy for the artist in pursuing subject matter that was outside her normal repertoire.

Berowra as a community struggled to make ends meet following the Great Depression; the luxury car of the Oldsmobile certainly stood out in the context of this small rural outpost. On Bill Foster's recommendation, the Prestons hired a young local man called Jack Overton as the full-time chauffeur and general roustabout. Their main housekeeper, Myra Worrell, recounted:

'Jack Overton was very young to be driving them [the Prestons] around. I think their car was an Oldsmobile. I suppose he didn't need a licence. It used to bump down Hillcrest, which was just big rocks and holes, like a creek bed, and he'd go round a big pine tree in the middle of the road to get in our gate'. [22]

Once well-known local resident Peter Huett in his vivid recollections stated that his father George Huett designed and constructed the pergola and garage at The Springs. George Huett had an outstanding reputation as the local builder within the district at the time. Moreover, 'Preston' was a familiar name in the Huett household as we know discussions did ensue regarding Huett's ongoing work at the Preston property.[23] Presumably, Huett also undertook the major renovations within the house, but there is no material evidence to support this idea.

'Beautiful Berowra' was the promotional catchcry for the suburb as an idyllic place to live. It was:

'a never-ending panorama of the finest land and water scenery in Australia … It is possible for anyone having daily occasions to attend to business in the city to reside in Berowra, train services meeting all requirements.'[24]

William Preston would have travelled by train each workday to his office in Kent Street, Sydney. Jack Overton drove Mr Preston in the Oldsmobile for the majority of the time to Hornsby station, some 10 kilometres closer to the city than Berowra station, perhaps to ease the burden of the journey into town each day. In the light of uncovering evidence that suggests the Prestons used the former Salmon's Garage, a bike shop in Hornsby, for storage purposes, this is highly probable, instead of taking the 7.30am train from Berowra Station, which arrived in the city about one hour later.[25] On returning to the property, Overton would wash and polish the car before garaging it. His other duties as instructed included clearing, building and preparation work. Despite his youth, Overton performed a vital role in helping to ensure the smooth running of the Preston household.

Mr Stinson, who was involved in a car-hiring business and worked as a gardener for a number of wealthy people at the time, became acquainted with the Prestons. He took over from Jack Overton as the full-time gardener and tended to the rose garden with his utmost attention and care. Planted in a tiered construction, framed by ironbark sleepers,[26] the rose garden viewed from the verandah made a spectacular and colourful display. In 2005, on a field trip to where Myra Payne once lived on the poultry farm in Cowan, local artist David Lever and I came across an old rose bush, which made us think of Margaret Preston and her once splendid rose garden.

Housekeepers

Margaret Preston was rarely seen in the Berowra community, but her presence was known and acknowledged at the time. Preston preferred to remain reclusive and spent 'a lot of time in the garden and in the bush and doing her artwork of course.[27] Her art practice was a primary and active process sustained by the quiet rural atmosphere where Preston experienced little disruptions. With the unwavering support of her husband, Preston thrived in this environment, working in a range of mediums from painting and printmaking to sewing, creating postcards (yet to be recovered) and a range of craft work. Domestic responsibilities and the 'ordered routine of her house'[28] were assigned to hired help. The best known was Myra Payne, nee Worrell.

Myra's mother with her daughters came to Sydney from the country and lived in Chatswood. In 1923, at 18 years of age, Myra Worrell first met Preston working in a shop at Mosman. The two women befriended each other and, soon afterwards, Myra went to live with the Prestons as their housekeeper. Their interactions were reminiscent of the lead characters drawn from Bernard Shaw's *Pygmalion* – Preston taught Myra how to speak and act in a 'proper' manner. She corrected Myra's speech and diction whenever she felt it faulted. Myra's demeanour was well suited for Preston – she was good-natured, loyal and hardworking. No doubt, Preston's coaching had a lasting influence on Myra, as local knowledge recounted her as being educated and well spoken.

Myra Worrell had modelled for both Preston and Thea Proctor as early as 1925. Preston was introduced to all of Myra's siblings: Iris, Una and Kate. Kate, the youngest sister, was the model for the silhouette nude by Preston titled *Nude 2*, held in the National Gallery of Australia collection. In 1925, Preston painted Myra as a confident new-age

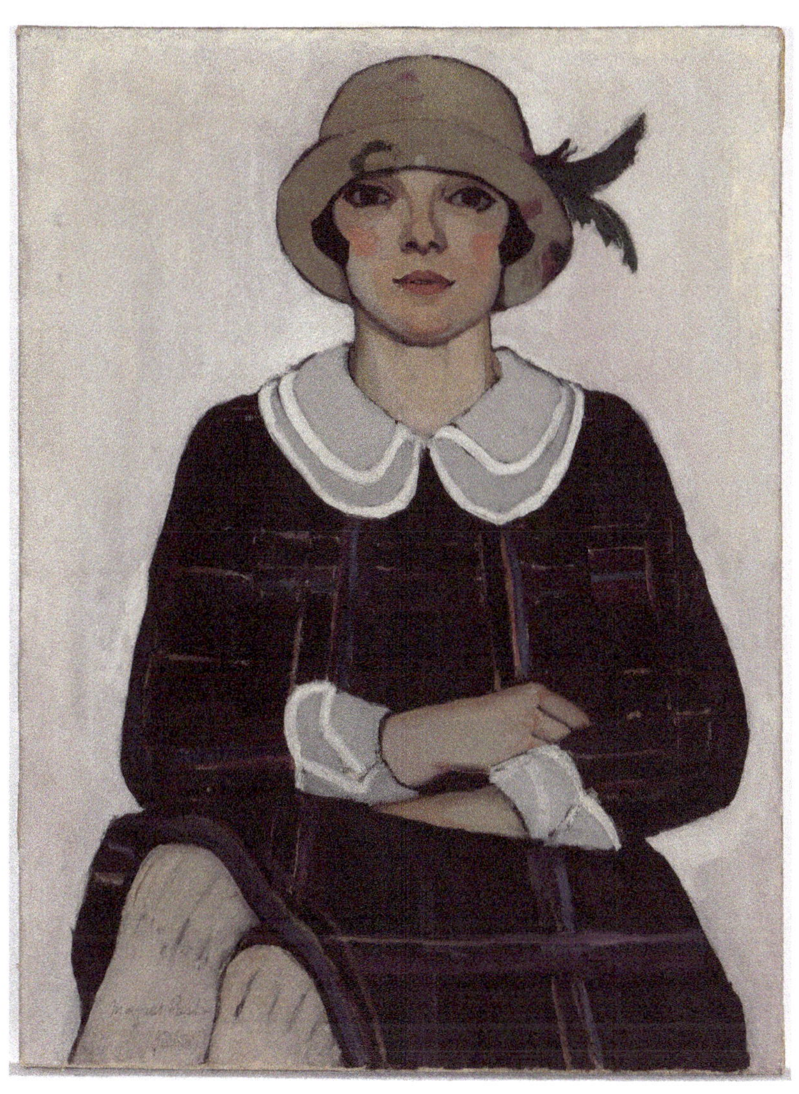

Preston's portrait of her maid Myra as *Flapper*, 1925.
Oil on canvas. National Gallery of Australia.

flapper. In its stark austerity, the painting made a bold statement capturing the essence of the modern woman. It defied the flapper stereotype in the clothes chosen for the sitting, not tight and glitzy but loose and stylish, more akin to a working outfit. In the picture, Myra with her large dark eyes stridently faces her onlookers in a graceful and defiant poise. Critics at the time, however, dismissed the painting as 'harsh and ugly',[29] which infuriated Preston, who gifted the artwork to Myra.[30] Preston seized the opportunity to also portray Una as a flapper during this period; unfortunately, to date the artwork has not resurfaced. It took another five decades for the painting featuring Myra, *Flapper* (1925), to re-emerge in the public domain. In 1985, Myra and her family took the painting for assessment to Artarmon Galleries. 'Myra enjoyed that day as she talked with the owner about the circle of artists she had contact with due to her association with Margaret Preston.'[31] Hailed as a rare and important portrait by Preston, the National Gallery of Australia purchased *Flapper* for the nation's permanent collection.

Myra accompanied the Prestons from the Mosman home to Berowra. By available accounts, she was a good cook, providing the Prestons with their required meals, especially the morning and afternoon tea services. She also attended guests staying at 'The Springs' such as the Ure Smiths, Will Ashton and others from Preston's art circles. Sydney Ure Smith, as President of the Society of Artists and a leading Australian art publisher who co-founded *Art in Australia* in 1916, was extremely influential. It was advantageous for Preston to pursue those networks in the promotion of her artwork and as an artist of note. Myra prepared meals using a fine assortment of fresh produce from local farms and what was available on the Preston property. She used a wood combustion No. 30. 'Courtier' stove, which remains a nostalgic presence in the home's current kitchen. A buzzer positioned in the Prestons' dining room to call upon the service of 'domestics' during mealtimes evidences the class divide of that period. Whether they were working in the kitchen or in the domestic quarters next door, the loud-sounding bell would inevitably reach them.[32] On what was Lot 59, containing the watercourse, a cottage was specifically built for the changing round of domestic staff and hired help the Prestons employed over a seven-year period. The house contained four small rooms and when guests stayed overnight, the domestic helpers were required to vacate the premises and retire to a self-contained single room.[33]

Myra Payne recalled how before the supply of electricity came to Berowra in 1937, 'the water [was heated] for the showers in a large wood copper'.[34] It seems the copper was also utilised for laundry duties. When the subsequent owners of the housekeepers' quarters purchased the house in 1991, they noted eight washtubs lined the backyard.[35] More than likely, the washtubs pertained to the Preston era, vestiges of the property's former life in accommodating so many guests on the weekends.

Myra Payne made lasting friendships with locals such as Bill Foster within the Berowra community. Bill's parents owned Fosters Store, the hubbub of Berowra and a place that sold just about everything, from milk, butter, bread and meat to clothing, roofing, washboards and roofing – 'It was like Anthony Horderns ... everything from a needle to an anchor.'[36] Bill worked as the delivery boy for his parents' store. Each day he would deliver by horse and cart essentials such as bread, butter, milk and meat to the Berowra community. Included in his daily run was the Preston household. Bill recalled:

'I was always greeted by Myra the maid at the back door. I never really spoke to Margaret Preston but I can remember her pottering around ... They had the phone connected to ring through the grocery order but I most often picked up the next day's order from Myra.'[37]

In 1934, Myra departed the Preston household to marry Walter Payne, a local poultry farmer and captain of the Berowra bush fire brigade. She went to live in nearby Cowan, where the couple with his sisters developed a modern poultry farm. Myra was hardworking and much admired among locals, affectionately remembered for driving her mighty Dodge truck to church each week. The loss of Myra's good housekeeping skills clearly upset Preston. The sense of order and routine

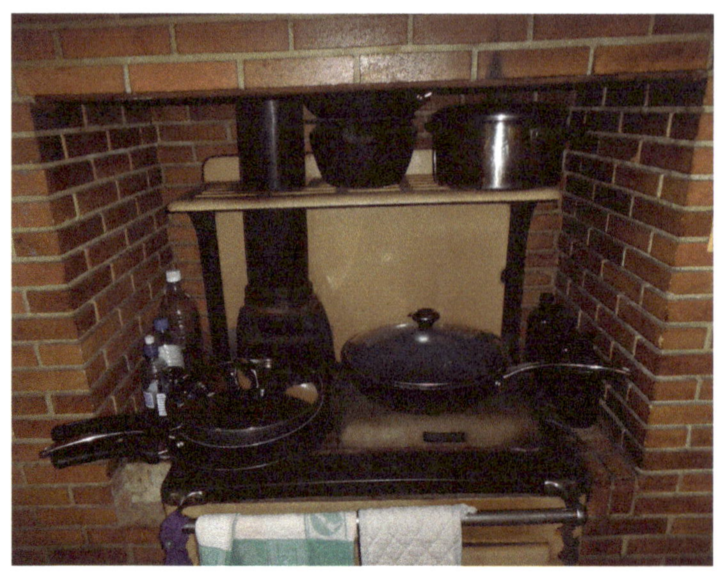

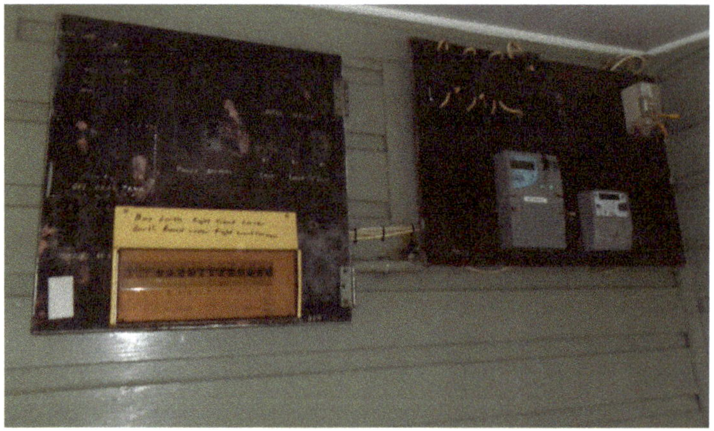

The original kitchen stove still stands, as does the original electrical wiring board (left) at 'The Springs'.

to her household upended, she exclaimed in a letter to John Young, 'I won't be in town for goodness knows when as I'm breaking in new domestics'. [38]

The next housekeeper hired by the Prestons was Doris Bell. She entered their employment sometime in 1934 and stayed with the Prestons until 1939. The correct etiquette and service of tea was important to Preston, and a variety of biscuits and cakes to accompany this ritual would have been expected. There is a wonderful entry submitted by Bell that evidences the making of fruit cracknels in the Preston kitchen. A simple, easy recipe that takes 6 to 8 minutes to bake in a moderate oven decorated with a 'thin slice of crystallised orange' won Miss D.M. Bell, c/o Mrs Margaret Preston, Berowra, NSW, a Consolation Prize of 2/6.[39] When Doris Bell left The Springs, she enlisted in the army.

The third and last house cleaner the Prestons hired for a brief period was a Lyn Izzard, who was reportedly married to the gardener, Mr Stinson, though evidence to support this has yet to be confirmed.

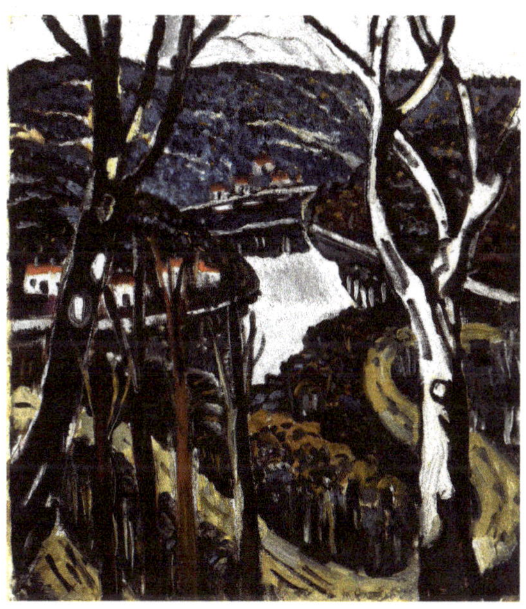

Berowra creek, 1943. Oil on canvas. National Gallery of Australia.

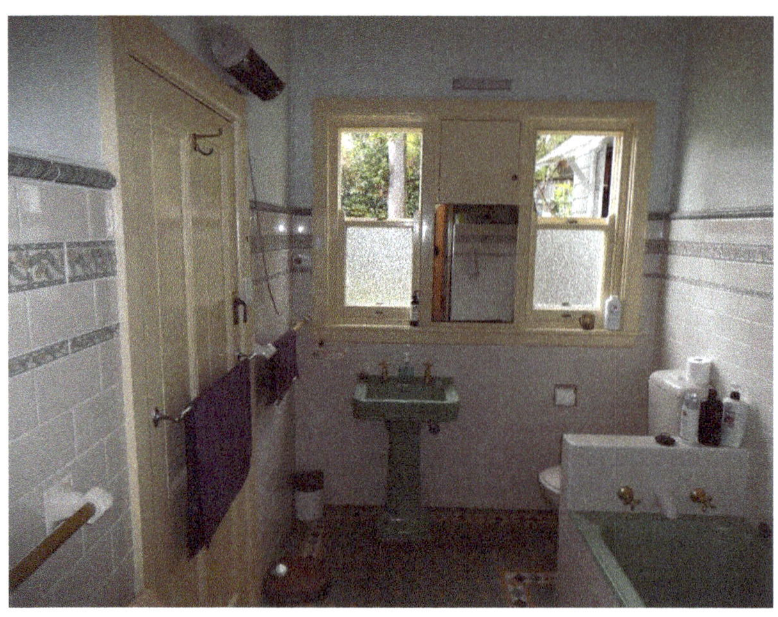

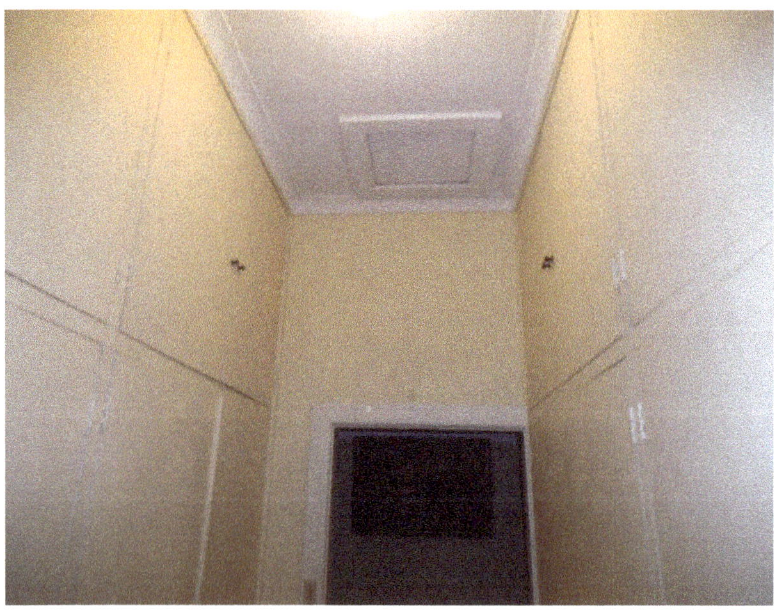

Original tiled bathroom (top), and double pantry in Preston's home.

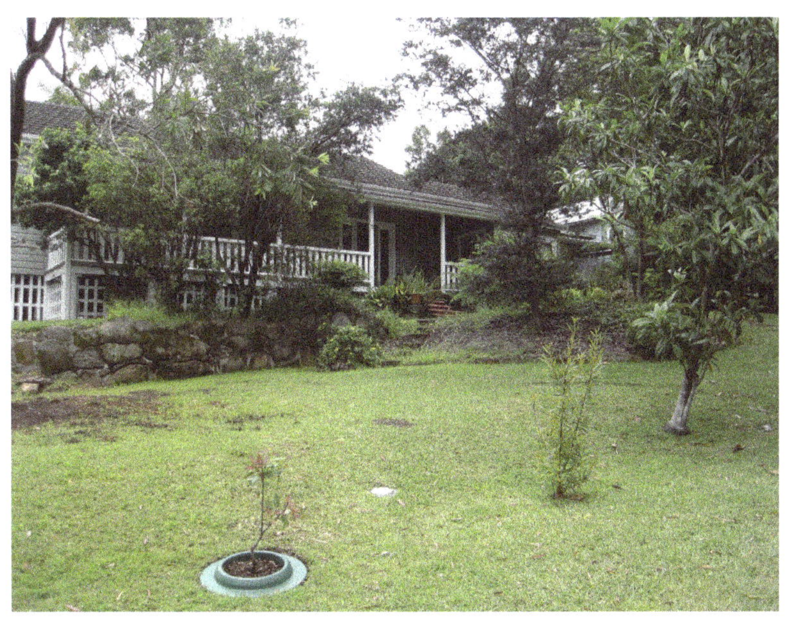

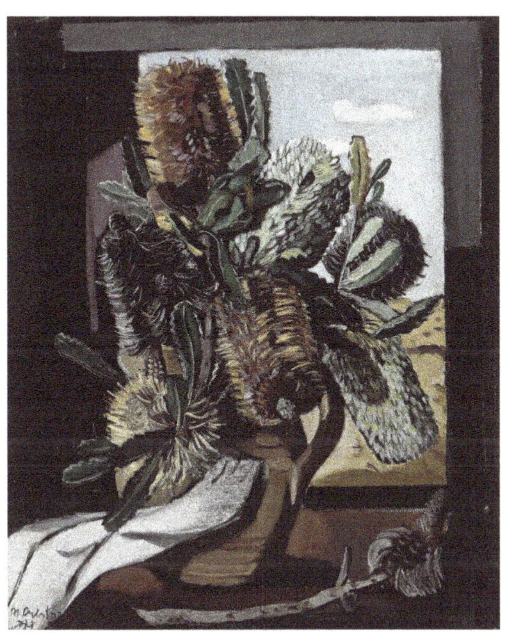

Preston's home as it is now.
Banksia on a Window Ledge, 1934.
Oil on canvas. Private Collection.

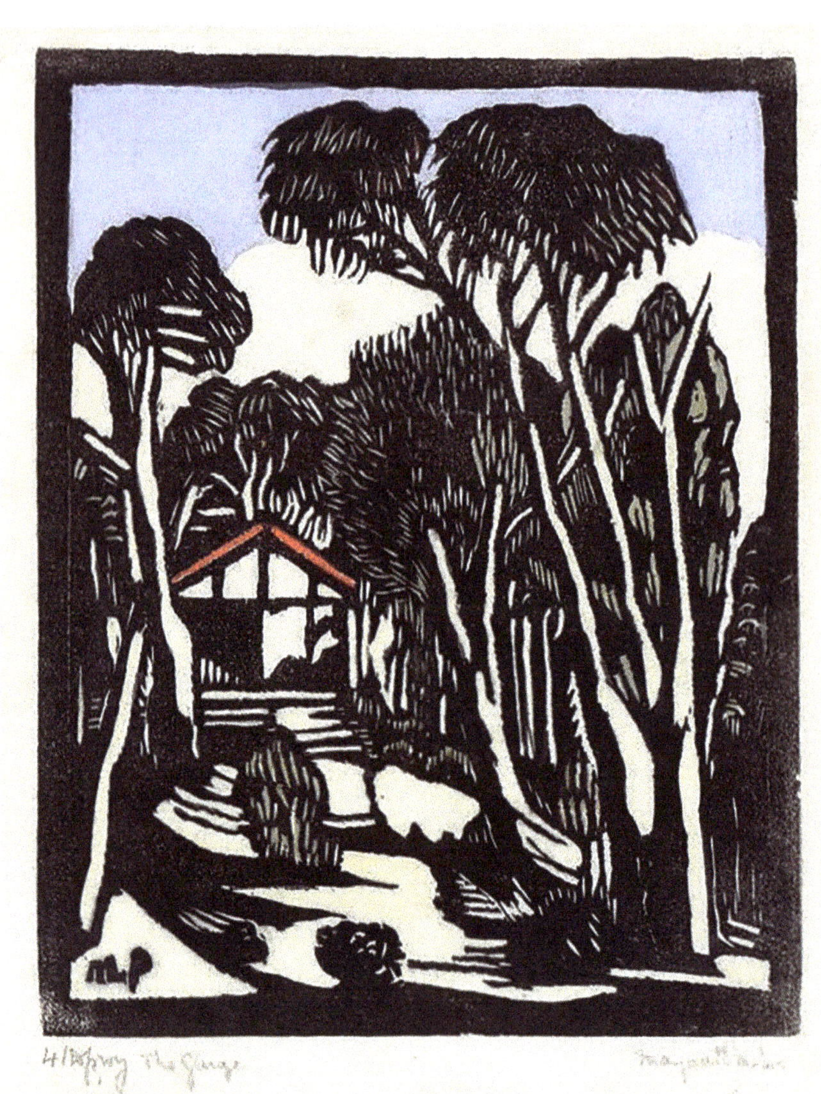

The garage, c. 1932. Hand-coloured woodcut. National Gallery of Australia.

Australian Rag Rugs

In 2005, the recovery of two magnificent rag rugs arguably produced by The recovery after decades in storage of two magnificent, hooked rag rugs in 2005, arguably produced by Preston while living at Berowra, encapsulates the natural world in connection to home and place. Removed from the hectic life she had led in the city, Preston delved into the decorative arts in making her Berowra home comfortably modern. Preston was certainly adept in producing a wide range of decorative art forms – from pottery and china painting to beadwork and basket making using materials such as wool, hessian, burlap, woolpack, raffia and string. She had an affinity for embellishing the aesthetic with the practical; demonstrated in a coverlet she made for an outdoor bed. 'I did mine with coloured string on woolpack and found them very practicable as they do not look "beddy", but smart, and are waterproof and keep out the dust as well'.[40] The attribution was not surprising given her aptitude for the decorative arts.

In the 'Eucalyptus rug', c. 1933, Preston produced a stylised depiction of the Western Australian gum blossom. She transformed the shape of the eucalyptus and flattened its foliage, fruit and trunk into a symmetrical structure, with the dark-green arcs infused with 'our own eucalyptus shape triangle leaf and its circular shaped flower'.[41] Graced with a vivid maroon colour derived from 1930s women's wool challis suiting, the flowers stand out and contrast with the selection of colours and textures. The tonal palette of red, greens, browns and grey with the shapes favoured with black outlines augments a three-dimensional effect. A stronger saturation of the green colour appears in small sections where Preston over-dyed those pieces. She knew about plant dyes and possibly experimented to that effect. The various cotton drills in navy, khaki, palace drills (fine-striped tweed) and mottled blanket material (tough and

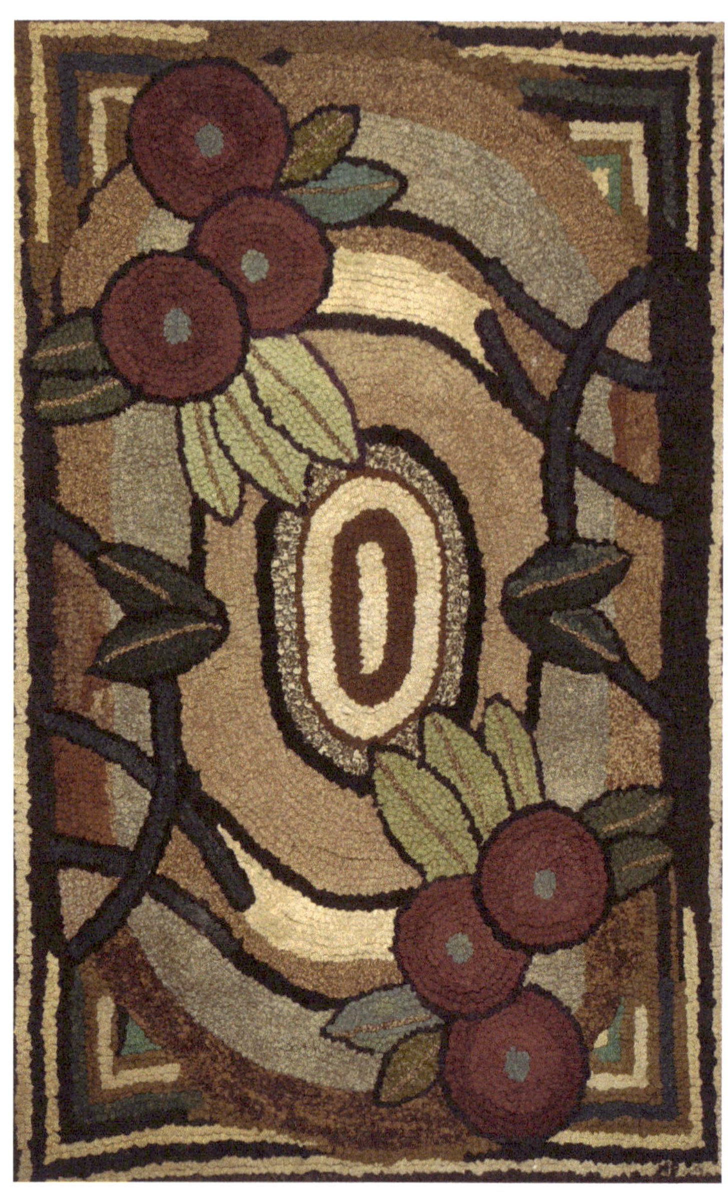

Margaret Preston's *Eucalyptus Rug*, 1933, based on her 1928 painting. National Gallery of Australia.

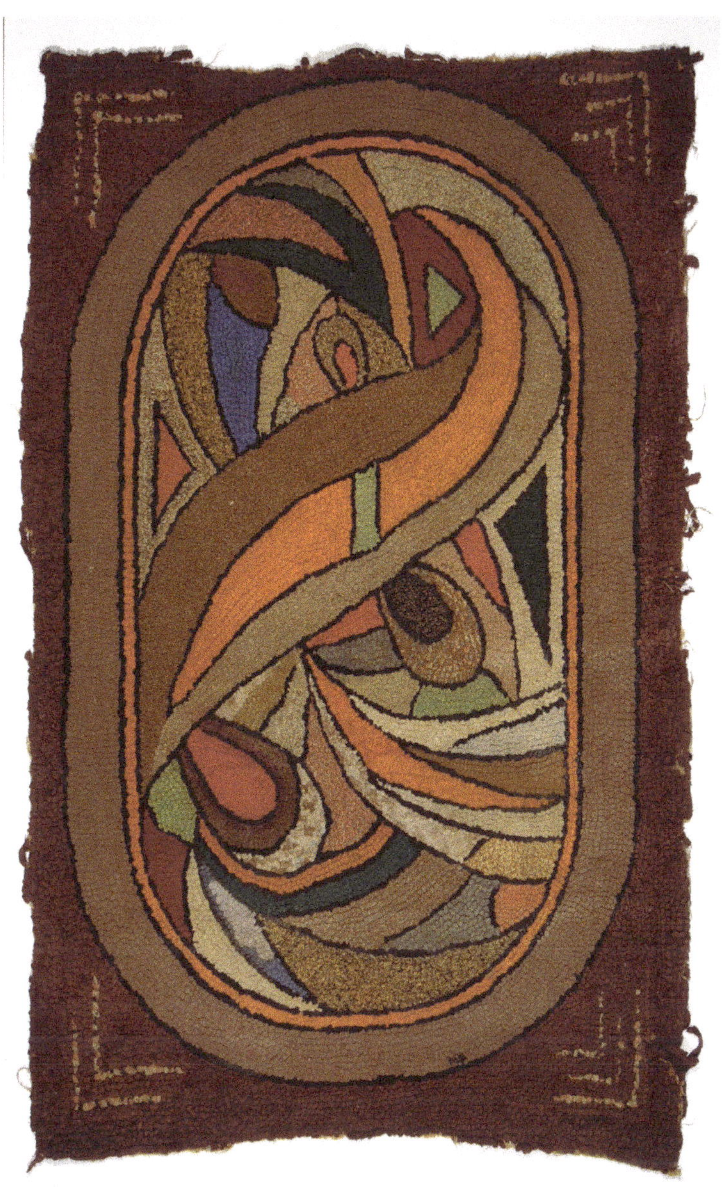

Margaret Preston's *Hakea Rug*. National Gallery of Australia.

non-fraying) furnished an intense colour range heightening the rugs' attractiveness.

The abstract rug referred as the 'Hakea rug', 1934, resembles the inner ecology of a hakea nut, which grew and continues to grow prevalently in Berowra. After fire, the hakea nut opens to expose a dazzling cedar-red internal and ovular structure. In the same year as the rug's making, Preston made a woodblock print based on the hakea. She used a specimen rather than sourcing it from its natural habitat. 'Mrs Steel has sent me some Hakea, so I'm hurrying to set a small block along by it. After that - To Tahiti - for 2 months at least'.[42] Returning from her overseas trip presumably reinvigorated, Preston embarked on producing this astonishing rug with the central motif largely based on the internal structure of the hakea nut.

The Hakea rug echoes aspects of the rhythmic pattern and verve of the artist Roy de Maistre's work titled *Rhythmic Composition in Yellow Green Minor,* 1919. The features are unquestionably striking in their similarities.[43] Perhaps relishing de Maistre's experimental work, a study in colour and movement, Preston applied a similar approach to the making of the Hakea rug. The broad sweeping movements punctuated by swirling symphonies of colour perfectly align and gesture within the abstracted forms.

The visual connection between the Hakea rug and Berowra Creek can be seen in the thick black outlines contained within Preston's woodblock print, *The winding road to Berowra waters*, 1939. The central spiralling motif, synchronised with forms converging and overlapping, creates a structure suggestive of the infamous winding road in its sharp bends, twists and surrounding deep crevices descending towards the waters. It represents a stylised bush motif with references to the river and ferry. The green band stands out from the rest of the design and 'was put there for a reason, a metaphorical reference for the ferry crossing the river.'[44] If the rug provides a direct link to Berowra Creek and surrounding bushland, expressing her deep fondness, the artist has left an enduring legacy to the sense of place and belonging of a regional outpost.

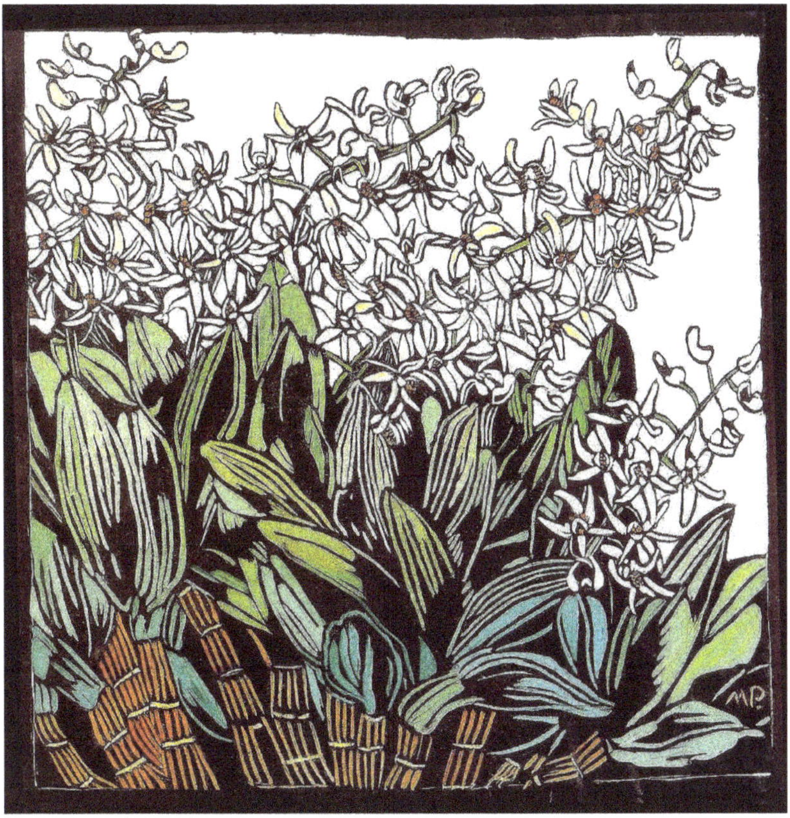

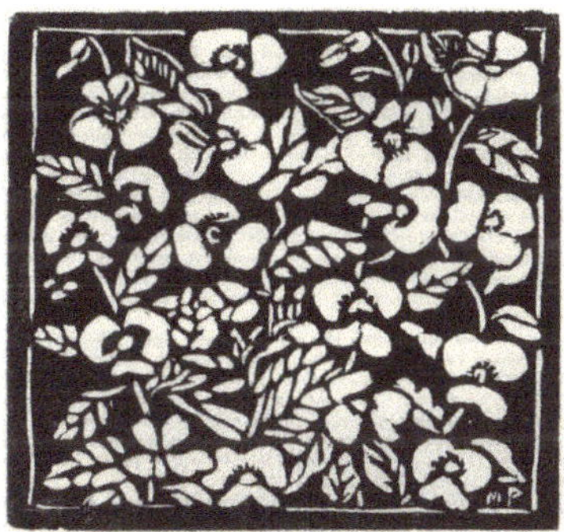

Australian Rock Lily, hand-coloured woodcut, c. 1933. Art Gallery of New South Wales. *Chorozema,* woodcut 1933. Published in *Manuscripts* no. 7, 1933.

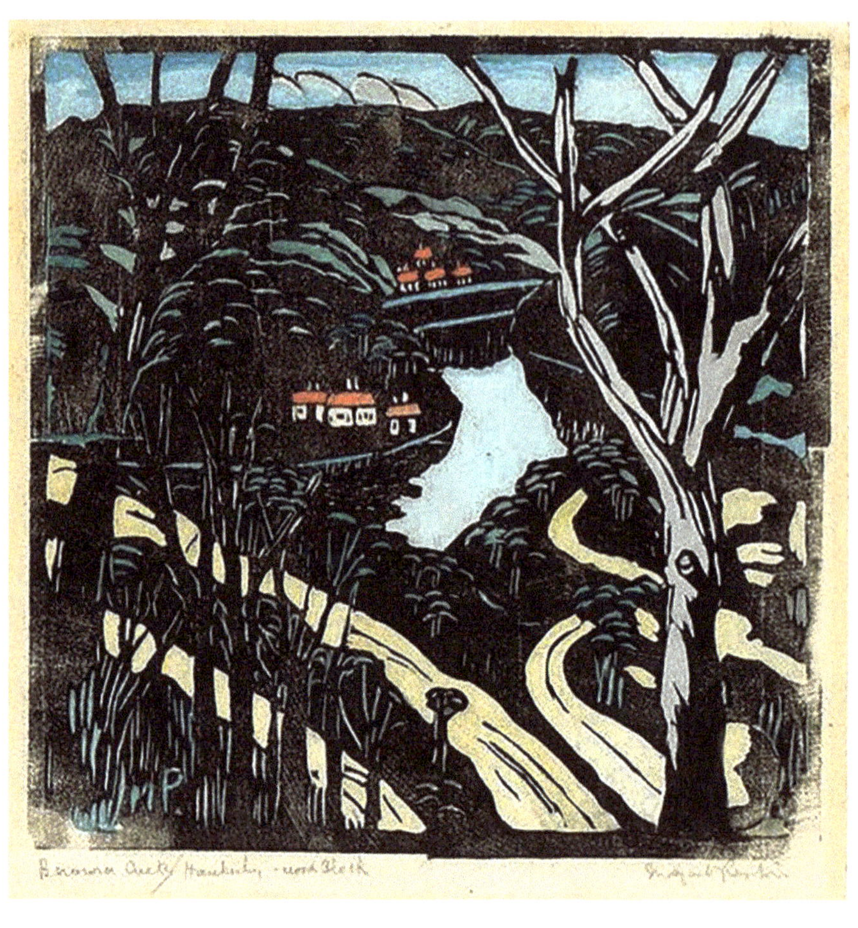

Margaret Preston, *The winding road to Berowra waters,* woodcut, c. 1939.
Art Gallery of New South Wales.

Local Modernism

The production of the rugs within the context of rural Berowra provides insights into the way regional variations played an important role in the developing story of Australian Modernism. As the historian, Humphrey McQueen, stated:

'the post-cubists were to make artistic forms by reconstructing the crudities of nature according to geometry. Yet, because nature was not the same everywhere and was altered by people, this universal problem for art required regional solutions suitable for each particular time.'[45]

The retreat to living in a small rural community afforded Preston the solitude and space for reflection, and in that, her search for a national art that intersected with the natural world laid within the place of Berowra. The difficulties she encountered with painting were resolved in craftwork; Preston, though, made no division between art and craft but considered the practices intertwined. Inadvertently, the choice of Preston using a folk-art tradition of rug hooking in producing her first known abstract work postulates how the decorative arts were key to the story of a local Modernism. The hybrid nature of the abstract rug demonstrates this factor by the way Preston harnessed a complex array of influences. The synthesis of the rustic nature of Berowra as place, with the visual complexity of Aboriginal rainforest shields, and spirals found in nature unified with post-cubism of overlapping planes and repeating motifs engendered the rug's visual cohesion. A triumphal achievement within a local environment, merging the local, national and international.

Process and production of rag rugs

The production of rag rugs using recycled materials increased during the Depression era in Australia. Cheap to make and materials readily sourced - a chaff bag, wool, recycled clothing, and a hooking instrument, such as a chisel-pointed piece of wood – the rugs provided warmth and colour on bare, cold floors. 'Women living in poorer circumstances or who made do with little, often made rag rugs with strips of old woollen clothing'.[46] By the wake of the post-war economic boom, the production of rag rugs reduced; they turned into tainted reminders of a family's former impoverished state.

Purportedly, Margaret learnt the art of rug hooking while assisting soldiers in rehabilitation during World War I at the Seale-Hayne Hospital in Devon, England. The program employed decorative arts as therapy in assisting soldiers' recovery. Back home, the Red Cross Society employed women with arts and crafts training in their rehabilitation program. The art therapy utilised by these women included the making of rag rugs, which was particularly popular among the wounded soldiers.[47]

In around 1915, Anthony Horderns store advertised its out-of-season sample fabrics recommended for making mats or wool rugs created 'in any colour to match your room, or a motto or the name of the (purchaser's) house'.[48] William Preston, as a co-director of Anthony Horderns, may well have brought home a selection of material for Preston to experiment.

However, for the hooked rugs Preston made she spared no expense, cutting the materials on the bias (oblique direction), allowing the 'give and stretch' of the fabric to enhance the manipulation. It is reasonable to assume that Preston actively pursued searching for the right fabrics, colours and textures expedient to her desires. Also, Anthony

Horderns advertised the 'latest designs in Woollen and Cotton Fabrics, made by the most reliable British Manufacturers' ranging from drills and suiting to shirting in woven strip designs and Scotch twill. This new range of fabrics possibly provided Preston with an unconstrained selection that would further enhance the production of the rugs in colour, tones and textures.

Preston used a multidimensional palette in the creation of the rugs that allowed for greater plasticity. The rugs contain various fibres of cardigans, mottled jersey wool knits and blends, cotton drills and hand knits, the burnt orange vibrancy of 1920s overlocked jerseys, the thickness of lisle stockings and the stretch of 1920s and 30s swimwear, creating an interface to their precision making. The swimwear fabrics comprising a range of opulent and dazzling colours were a standout choice. Bathers came in blues, blacks, greens and an eye-catching hot pink. An overlocking technique employed to the bathing material prevented fraying, making the fabric ideal for rug making. The pre–World War II jersey knits were a pliable and more modern alternative to wool. The manipulation of form, space and chroma by Preston enhanced her technique through this careful selection of materials. Her astute choice of using new rather than recycled materials differentiate the rugs' production as innovative for the period.

Preston used chaff bags commonly found on farms as the surface, with the burlap hemmed at both ends and machine-stitched for preservation and stability. The cut-up materials pushed and pulled through by a hooking instrument into the closely woven burlap required a forceful hand. We know Preston acquired great strength and dexterity in her hands from all the woodblock printing she undertook. Preston would have firstly hooked-in the design proceeded by the background. This hooking method formed a loop one-quarter of an inch high on the rug's upper surface to create a thick, evenly textured, smooth pile.

At her Mosman home, before moving to Berowra, Preston had executed her designs on mats with chalk.

'The mats in my house were black mohair. After very little use they became worn-looking. The backs being made of a kind of canvas I took some chalk and drew on them the few simple lines of the design and filled them in with raffia. The worn side I covered with some bright, strong material. The result is that I have two jolly mats that are gay and original'.[49]

Chalk was also the preferred medium used for drawing on burlap in the making of rugs. Presumably, the execution and design drawn freehand onto the surface, with the central design hooked-in followed by the background was the process Preston followed. Myra Worrell was an accomplished sewer, who possessed a Singer sewing machine. There is a strong possibility Myra helped Preston in the cutting phase of the fabrics, it being a somewhat laborious task.

The rugs exude in colour, texture and design and rank with the fashion of the early decades of the last century. Material from women's and men's tailored suits acquired from Mark Foy's and David Jones are featured within the rugs. Preston experimented in design and mixing of materials – in standard rug hooking you will not see the mix of materials that Preston was willing to use. Unbridled by convention, she coalesced wools, tweeds and jerseys. The meticulousness applied to the rugs in design and production is unmatched. The confident manipulation Preston applied to the contrasting materials and textures produced two outstanding, evenly piled rugs.

New insights about the role of decorative design in Australia

The rugs provide new insights into the way decorative design was integral to the origins and subsequent evolution of abstraction within Australia. Preston, undoubtedly influenced by the context of place in a specific, local environment – removed from the distractions of the city – allowed her practice to expand and thrive under these conditions. She experimented with international idioms within a local setting. A reappraisal of the links between internationalism, nationalism and the important role the local plays within universal frameworks of Modernism is yet to be fully realised. A close study of Margaret Preston's range of artistic outputs in Berowra may lead to the publication of new findings in this area; a portrait that will constitute those rare transactions she encountered in the bush and Berowra Creek she most often visited. Preston's artworks of Berowra Creek and Calabash Bay are key indicators of the internal structures she was building towards localised, geographically bound art forms that largely originated from her craftwork and immediate surrounds. I will extend on that idea for another publication in the analysis of artworks specifically produced at Berowra that validates this proposition.

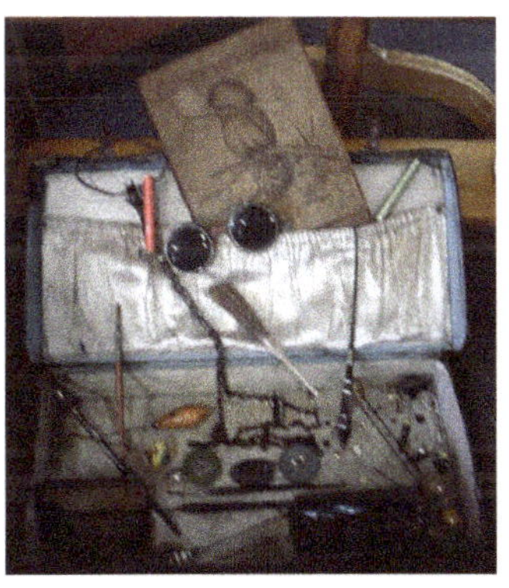

Margaret Preston's painting and craft kit as used in Berowra.

Painting Outdoors

The maelstroms of the Berowra bush and garden were the energy force that realised some of Preston's most ambitious paintings. In 1937, the Orient Company commissioned Preston to paint four panels of native flowers to adorn the verandah café walls of its new steamer, *Orcades*. An important commission for Preston, she acquired red gum blossoms all the way from Western Australia since the New South Wales gums had finished flowering. The journey required the flowers to be transported in ice, and on their arrival at the Berowra property Preston had to act swiftly. 'Of course, it was necessary to paint the flowers almost immediately before they wilted.'[50] The remaining flowers she obtained directly from her beloved Berowra garden. This led Preston to paint the commission largely outdoors on the estate. *The Daily Telegraph* reported: "Some I had to paint out in the open", Mrs. Preston said, for there "their colors are most vivid".[51]

The production of the four panels resplendent with native flowers represented a major feat. Two of the panels comprise gum blossoms, mixed with her favourite banksia and coral flowers; and the other two are filled with mixed flowers. Painted with vigour and determination, the massed bunches spill over the vases that express tactile openness and confidence of the artist pushing herself with an urgency to get the commission completed on time. Preston confided, 'The work was nothing if not erratic, sometimes taking me long hours of study, and other times having to be rushed. NO IMPRESSIONISM.'[52] These astoundingly beautiful artworks will always retain an indelible connection to Berowra in reimagining Preston painting those massed bunches of flowers from her garden.

The Berowra home stood at the threshold of Preston rediscovering native flowers in their natural habitat. An awakening for her palette, but also a different source of energy, light and context became injected into her overall practice. She no longer succumbed to making art as representational, but a heightened sense of reality began to touch her works existing in the time and place of its creation.

The painting Preston casually holds when photographed standing under the pergola unwittingly reveals one of her painting spaces, the skillion roof verandah. 'I expect I must be one of the few artists who, although they have a studio, prefer to work all over the house. I nearly drive my family mad!'[53] The verandah, enclosed on one side, allowed Preston to work in all sorts of weather conditions and still conveyed the features of being outdoors. 'The addition of a couple more lengths of verandah – one enclosed as a sleep-out and sewing room, and also equipped with holland curtains and covers, she has the ideal country home.'[54] The weatherboard exterior of the house revealed in this picture is the sole evidence indicating the original outside of the house. To contemplate the way Preston's much-utilised verandah she used as a studio space was featured in an unattributed artwork that has not seen the light of day since this photograph was taken some 80 years ago, narrates another mystery. What is absorbing is the vista Preston looked out on from this vantage point, floating into the expanse of the sky and where, for a moment, time stood still for Preston. 'I live up here so quietly that it seems as if I'd been on a volcano & got blown up.'[55]

The Sydney Morning Herald had reported that the Prestons planned to retire in Berowra: 'Mrs Margaret Preston, the artist, who has chosen this quiet and idyllic spot in which to retire from the hubbub of city life and do her work in the calm security of the Australian bush'. But the couple's original intention did not eventuate; their plan was severely disrupted by the impending war about to erupt. By the beginning of World War II, Berowra Waters was considered an entry point, increasing the fears and vulnerability among locals. No doubt, the Prestons felt an anxiety in the area's isolation and decided to leave Berowra and return to Mosman. The property was sold to Thomas Sydney Smith of Vaucluse, listed as an investor, on 10 August 1939. In the following month, the United Kingdom declared war on Germany. Berowra's population in April of that year was recorded at just 351; a sparsely populated community.

The years spent at Berowra were a transitional period in Margaret Preston's life and artistically she thrived within this environment. Preston's Berowra artworks respond to the energy she sought after her fright with 'looking over the edge', an extension and consolidation of her observational powers in touching the reality and wonders of nature. On the outskirts, the universal met with the local meshed with the home and the natural world. Margaret Preston's Berowra home and art conjure those rare, picturesque and poetic moments of time, space and inimitable memories.

Rhonda Davis
Berowra, November 2021

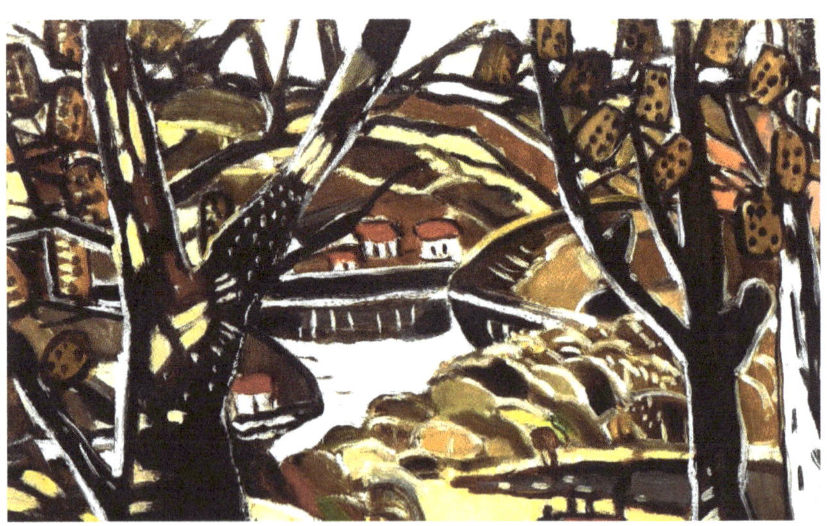

I Lived at Berowra, 1941 (detail).Oil on canvas. Art Gallery of New South Wales.

Acknowledgements

Special thank you and acknowledgement to my long-time friend David Lever for all his ongoing support, encouragement and with his astute advice and research have been invaluable in realising the Margaret Preston in Berowra project.

To the wonderful Tom Thompson the publisher and editor of this book for his ongoing encouragement and support.

To the late Bill Foster, the late Peter Huett and the late Pam Gartung, in acknowledgement of their contribution, sharing their stories that greatly assisted the project back in 2005.

Special thank you to Garry and Cathy Smith for their unwavering support and hospitality they have showed the team over the years.

Sincere thanks to Robyn Berkovic, Rhonda Coleman, Shirley Collins, Neil Davis, Robyn Ellison and Ann Lomas without their support the project would not have taken the direction it did.

Jacqui Stone for her meticulous proof reading and suggestions of the text.

To the artists that participated in the initial exhibition project back in 2005 and their continued support towards the research of Margaret Preston in Berowra, Effy Alexakis and Juno Gemes.

To most of all, my beloved late husband the artist Mark Davis, forever in our thoughts.

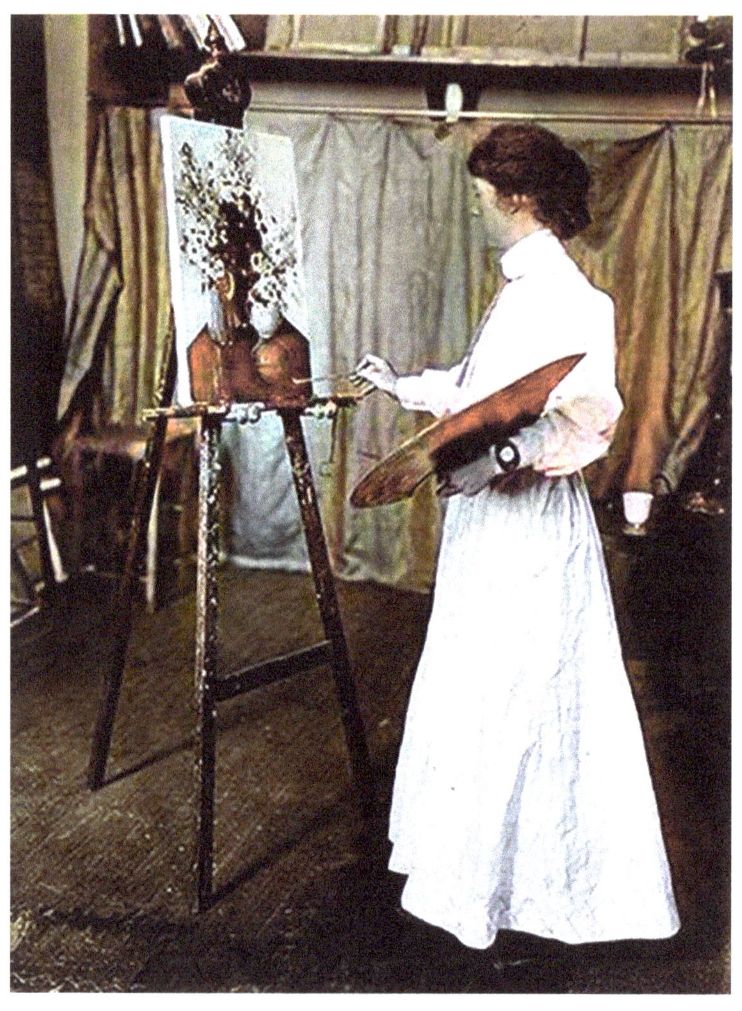

Margaret McPherson painting in her Adelaide teaching studio, 1909.

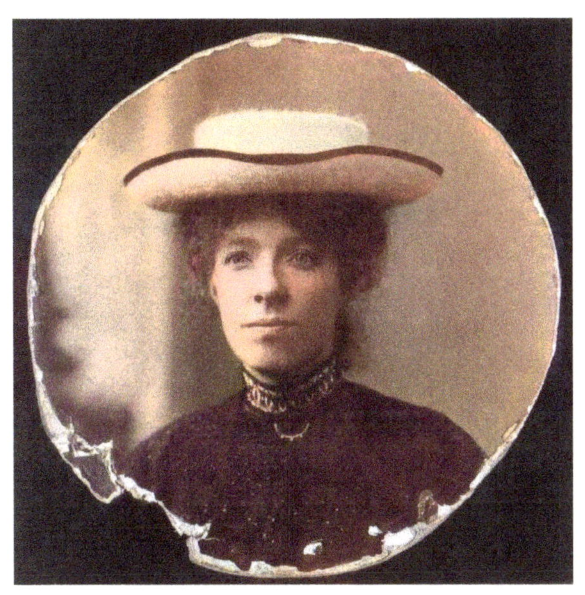

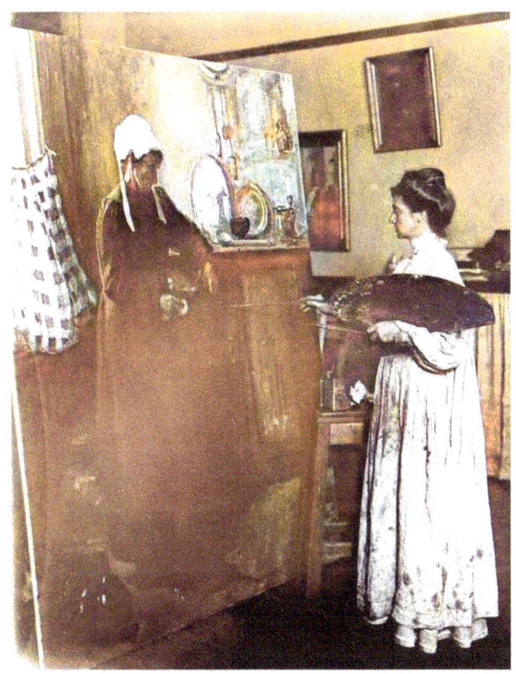

Margaret Rose McPherson, Adelaide 1894.
Bessie Davidson, working on *The Servant*, Adelaide 1909.

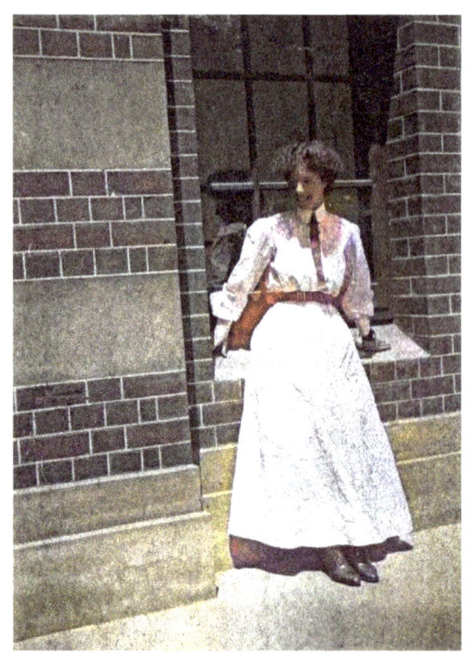

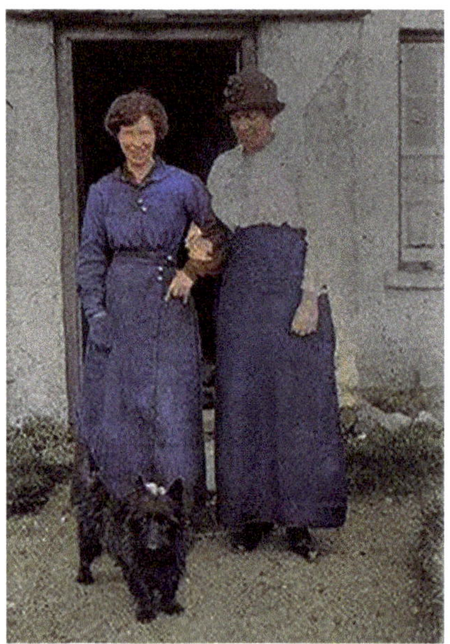

Margaret McPherson in Paris 1905.
McPherson with Gladys Reynell, and Little Jim, 1915.

TIMELINE

1875 - Margaret Rose McPherson (MRM) was born on the 29th April, in Port Adelaide to parents David McPherson, a Scottish marine engineer, and Prudence McPherson.

1885 - MRM and family move to Sydney where MRM attended Fort Street Girls School for two years.

1889 - MRM at the National Gallery of Victoria Art School under Frederick McCubbin, till 1894.

1896 - MRM in Adelaide due to father's illness. Following his death she returns to the National Gallery of Victoria Art School, studying under Bernard Hall.

1897- MRM wins the Still Life Scholarship.

1898 - MRM continued her studies at the Adelaide School of Design, under H.P. Gill and Hans Heysen.

1899 - MRM established her own teaching studio in Adelaide's AMP Building

1903 - MRM's mother Prudence died.

1904 - MRM travels to Europe with Bessie Davidson.

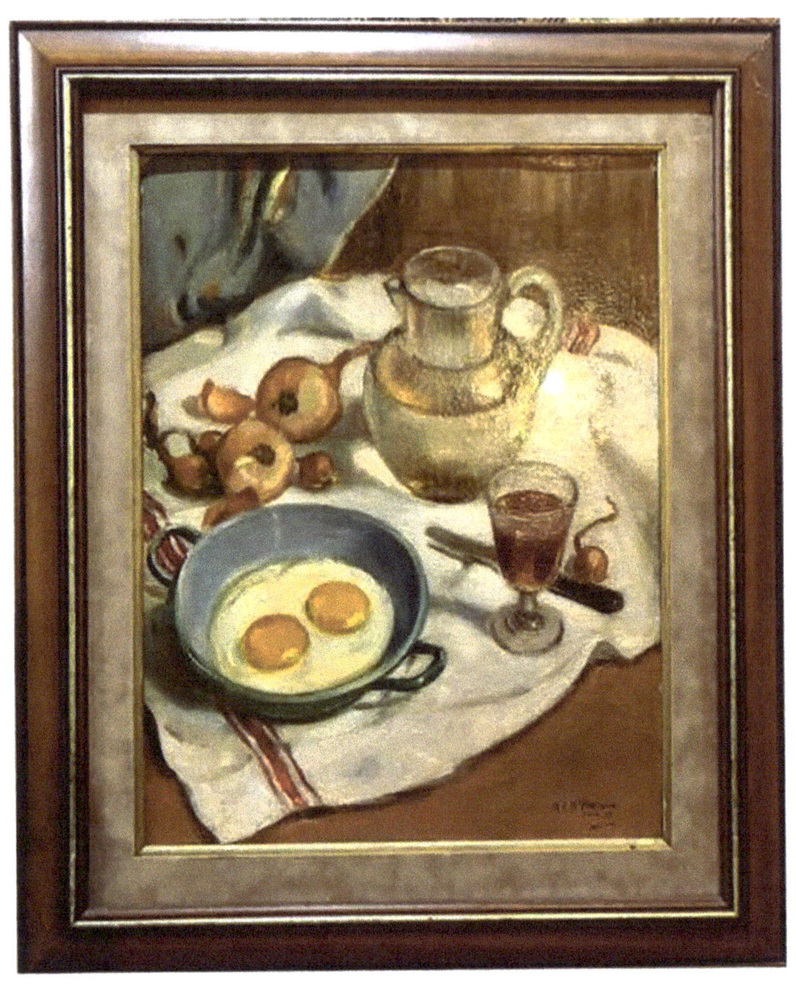

La Cuisine (nature morte) aka *The Kitchen*
Oil on canvas, 55 x 43 cm
Signed and dated lower right, 'M. R. McPherson/Paris 1913'
Painted in Paris, des Beaux-Arts Salon stamp to reverse.
Private Collection.

1905 - Studies at the Government Art School for Women in Munich, then MRM studies with Jules Levebre at 2 Rue Brea, Paris and exhibits a Still Life (Onions) at the Société Nationale des Beaux-Arts (SNBA).

1906 - MRM exhibits Le Chiffonnier (the Ragman) and a Still Life (Flowers) at the SNBA, and returned with Davidson to Adelaide on 15 December.

1912 - MRM travels to Paris with Gladys Reynell on 8 February, and studied design at Roger Fry's Omega Workshops in London, moving to Paris in April and being in contact with Bessie Davidson and Rupert Bunny.

1913 - MRM living at 64 Rue Madam, Paris, exhibits a Still Life - *Novembre sur le balcon* at the SNBA. Stays on the Ile de Noirmoutier, off Brittany in June and July.

1914 - MRM exhibits *La Cuisine (The Kitchen)* at the SNBA, and moves to London with Reynell.

1915 - MRM takes students for intensive study at Bunmahon, Ireland.

1916 - MRM and Reynell attended London's Camberwell School of Arts and Crafts to study pottery. MRM and Reynell teach shell-shocked soldiers craft at the Seale-Hayne Neurological Military Hospital in Devonshire.

1919 - MRM and Reynell leave for Adelaide to arrange joint exhibition. MRM married Lieutenant William George Preston on 31 December in Adelaide.

1920 - Prestons move at the Ritz Hotel, Cremorne, then to a flat in 'Glenorie', Musgrove Street, Mosman.

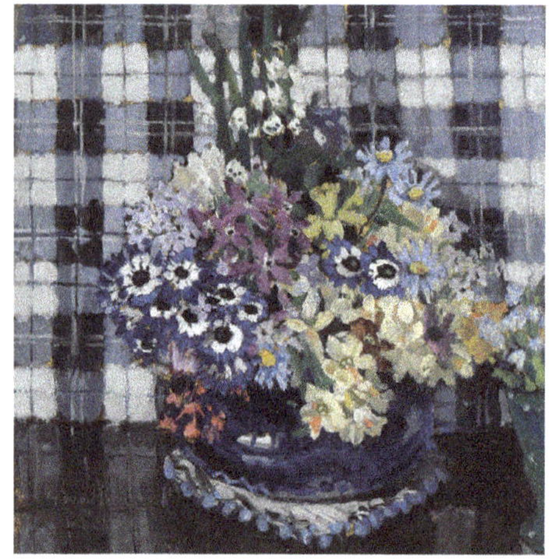

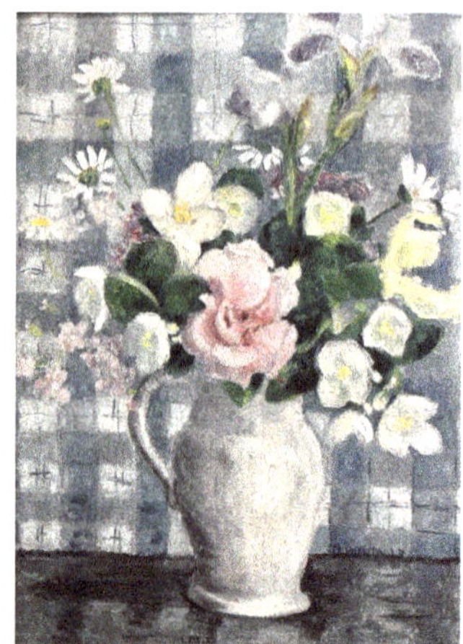

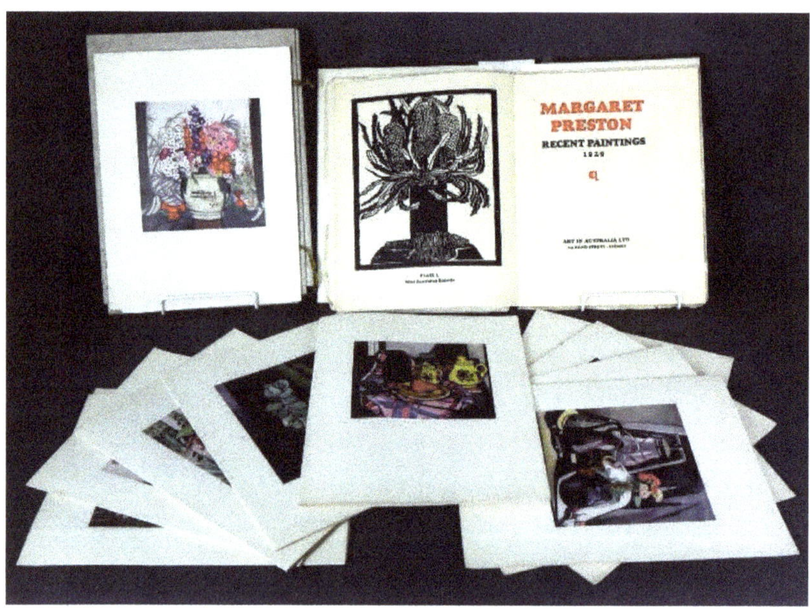

Still Life, 1922, oil on canvas. Private Collection.
(Still-Life), 1923, oil on canvas. Private Collection.
Recent Paintings, portfolio as published 1929.

1922 - Prestons move to 11 Park Avenue Mosman.

1927 - Margaret Preston Number of *Art in Australia* published by Art in Australia, 3rd Series, no. 22.

1929 - *Margaret Preston Recent Paintings* published by Ure Smith, in an edition of 250 copies.

1930 - Berowra is connected by a trunk line to Sydney and cottage Point Post Office.
MP: The Application of Aboriginal Designs, in *Art in Australia,* 3rd Series, no. 31 (March).
MP: Away With Poker-Worked Kookaburras and Gumleaves, in *Sunday Pictorial,* 6 April.
MP: Pottery as a Profession, in *Art in Australia,* 3rd Series, no. 32 (June).
Wellington, New Zealand; 4 July to 2 August, *Exhibition by Leading Members of the Australian Society of Artists.*
Sydney, 5 September to 4 October, *Society of Artists Annual Exhibition,* Education Department's Art Gallery.
MP: Woodblocking as a Craft, in *Art in Australia,* 3rd Series, no. 34 (October).
Sydney, Nov 12-22 November, *The Contemporary Group,* 5th Annual Exhibition, Macquarie Galleries.
Sydney, December, *A Group of Decorative Artists,* Grosvenor Galleries.

1931 - MP: Art Gallery of Wanganui, in *Art in Australia*, 3rd Series, no. 36 (February).
Sydney, 14-28 May, *Society of Artists, Special Exhibition*, David Jones Restaurant Annex.
Berowra land lot 59 including 'The Springs' transferred to William Preston on 21 August 1931.

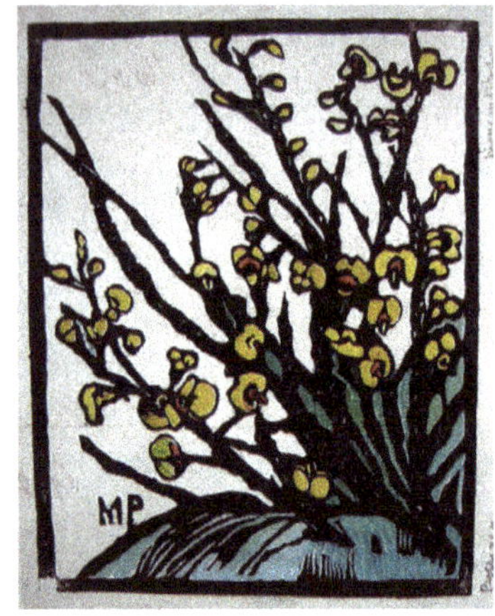

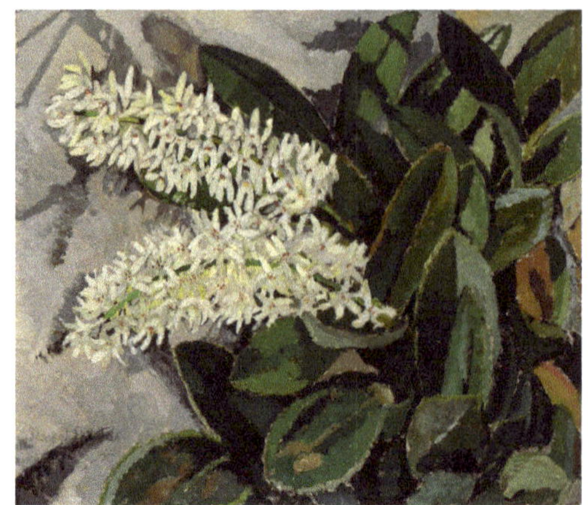

Bossiaea, hand-coloured woodcut, 1932. *Rock Lillies,* oil on canvas, 1932.

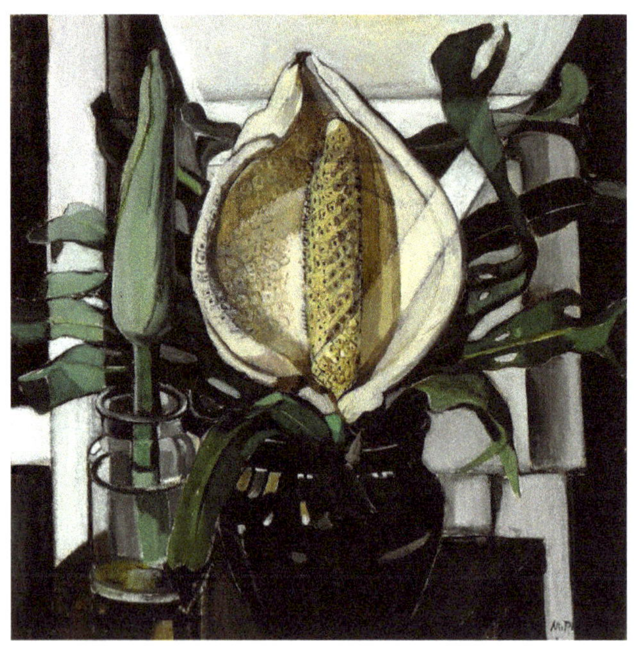

The Monstera Deliciosa, oil on canvas, 1934.

1931 - Sydney, 5 September to 2 October, *Society of Artists, Annual Exhibition*, Education Department's Art Gallery.

Berowra ferry is converted to power operation on 12 September.

The Empire Fair is opened at the new Berowra Cabaret roadhouse in November.

Sydney, 17 December onwards, *Christmas Exhibition*, Grosvenor Galleries.

1932 - Arthur Lubeck's 'Enterprise' conveys tourists on Berowra Waters.

Berowra's first petrol station built by Viv Lawless opposite the railway station.

Perth, 8 to 24 March, *Exhibition of Australian Art*, Boards Ltd. Sydney, 21 March to 3 April, *Sydney Harbour Bridge Celebrations*, Education Department's Art Gallery

Berowra land lot 60 transferred to William Preston on 29 March 1932.

MP: Meccano as an Ideal, in *Manuscripts*, no. 2 (June).

MP: Basket Weaving for the Amateur, in *Home*, 13, no. 8 (August).

Sydney, 2 to 30 September, *Society of Artists, Annual Exhibition*, Education Department's Art Gallery

Melbourne, 1 to 7 November, *Work by Four Artists*, 52a Collins Street.

Sydney, 2 to 14 November, *The Contemporary Group*, 7th Annual Exhibition, Macquarie Galleries.

1933 - MP: An Exhibition 1933, in *Manuscripts*, no 4 February).

The Huetts operate Berowra Waters ferry (to 1936).

Sydney, 8 September to 6 October, *Society of Artists, Annual Exhibition*, Education Department's Art Gallery.

Melbourne, 12 September to ?, *Exhibition of Etchings, Woodcuts Etc*, Sedon Galleries.

Sydney, 24 October to 6 November, *Contemporary Group Exhibition,* Farmer's Blaxland Galleries.

Melbourne, 27 October to 11 November, *Australian Art Association, Annual Exhibition*, Athenaeum Gallery.

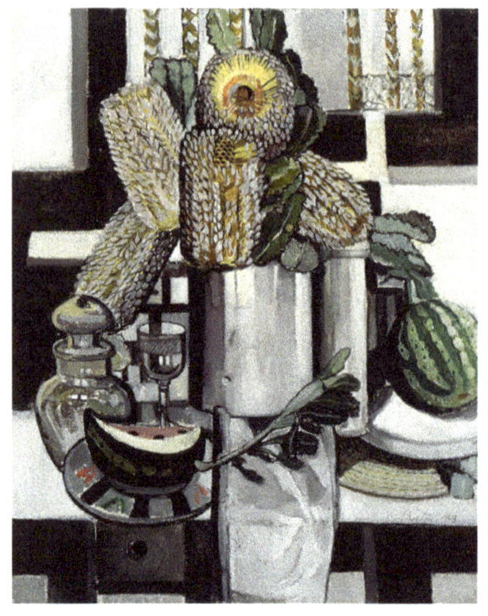

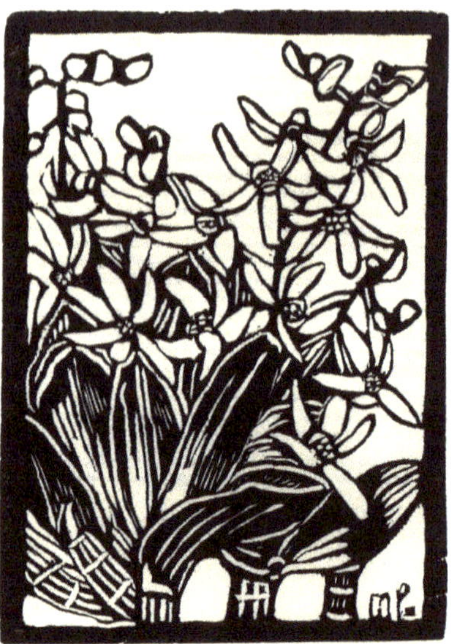

Native Honeysuckle, 1933, oil on canvas. *Australian Rock Lily*, 1933, woodcut.

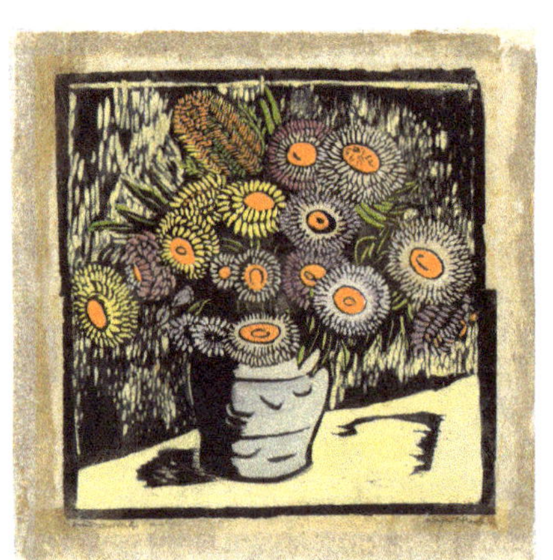

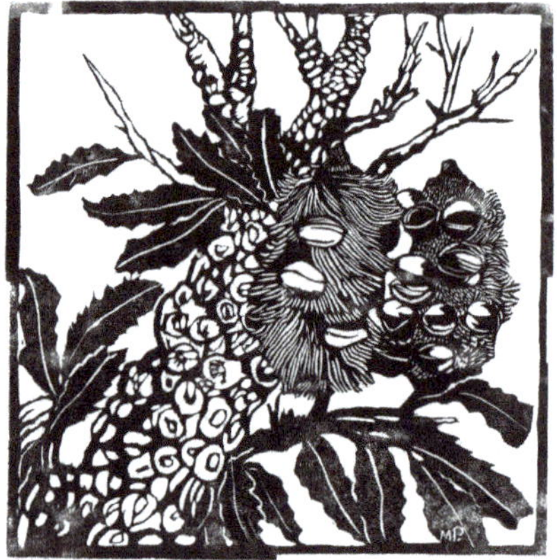

Native Everlastings, 1935, hand-coloured woodcut. *Banksia and Trunk,* 1935, woodcut.

1933 - MP: Just a Tour of the Islands, in *Home* 14, no. 11 (November).
Melbourne, 12 to 24 December, *Exhibition of Etchings, Woodcuts and Pencil Drawings,* Sedon Galleries.

1934 - Melbourne, 29 May to 9 June, *Exhibition of Etchings, Pencil Drawings and Woodcuts,* Sedon Galleries.
Sydney, 12 to 25 July, *Women Artists of Australia Exhibition,* Education Department's Art Gallery.
Sydney, 14 to 25 August, *Contemporary Group Exhibition,* Farmer's Blaxland Galleries.
Sydney, 7 September to 5 October, *Society of Artists, Annual Exhibition,* Education Department's Art Gallery.
Berowra: Myra Worrell, Preston's housekeeper for 12 years, leaves to marry local Berowra man, Walter Payne, receiving two Preston designed rugs noted herein as 'Hakea' and 'Eucalyptus'.
Melbourne, 8 October to ?, *Centenary Art Exhibition,* Commonwealth Bank Chambers.
Adelaide, 26 October to 17 November, *South Australian Society of Arts, Spring Exhibition,* Institute Building.

1935 - MP: Nothing but the East, in *Home,* 16, no. 1 (January).
MP: Peiping and the Great Wall, in *Home* 16, no. 2 (February).
MP: The Puppet Show of Osaka, in *Manuscripts,* no. 12 (February).
Berowra Waters Progress Association formed.
Sydney, 3 to 30 May, *Women's Industrial Art Society,* Education Department's Art Gallery.
Melbourne, 9 to 30 July, *Contemporary Group Exhibition,* Athenaeum Gallery.
Sydney, 13 to 24 August, *Contemporary Group Exhibition,* Farmer's Blaxland Galleries.

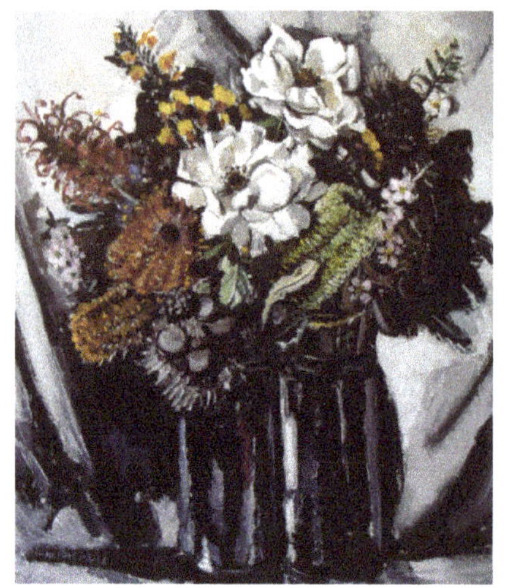

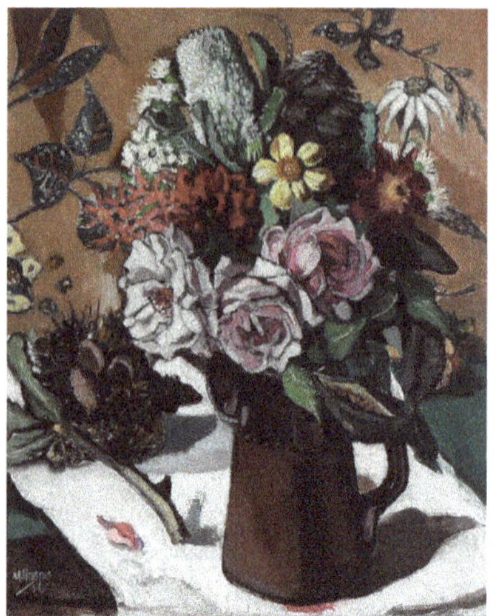

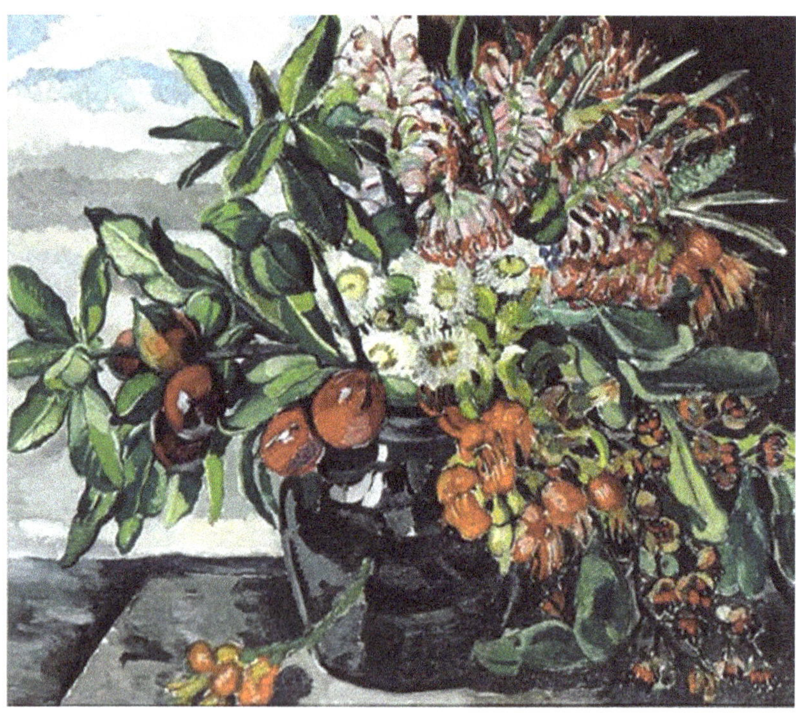

Still Life with Banksia, 1936 (top left) Private Collection;
Rose and Banksia, 1936 (top right)Art Gallery of New South Wales;
Australian Wildflowers, 1937, Private Collection. All oil on canvas.

1935 - Sydney, 6 September to 4 October, *Society of Artists, Annual Exhibition*, Education Department's Art Gallery.
Sydney, 9 October to ?, *Australian Painter-Etchers' and Graphic Arts Society Exhibition*, Farmer's Blaxland Galleries.
Melbourne, 3 to 24 December, *Exhibition of Etchings, Woodcuts, Etc.*,The Sedon Galleries.

1936 - Berowra Water swimming pool is built.
Sydney, February, *(Mixed Show)*, Macquarie Galleries.
Sydney, 20 to 31 July, *Contemporary Group Exhibition*, Farmer's Blaxland Galleries.
Melbourne, 11 to 22 August, *Contemporary Art Group*.
Sydney, August to October, *Margaret Preston Woodblocks*, Macquarie Gallery.
Sydney, 4 September to 2 October, *Society of Artists, Annual Exhibition*, Education Department's Art Gallery.
Melbourne , 9 to 24 December, *Exhibition of Etchings, Woodcuts, Etc.*, The Sedon Galleries.

1937 - 'Margaret Preston at home', *Australian Home Beautiful*, 1 February.
Electricity comes to Berowra Railway Station.
London, 8 to 29 May, *Exhibition of Paintings... by Artists of the British Empire*, Royal Institute Galleries.
Brisbane, 19 may to 5 June, *Society of Artists, Brisbane Exhibition*, Parbury House.
Exposition Internationale, Australian Pavilion, Paris.
Sydney, 5 to 19 August, Group Exhibition, Grosvenor Galleries.
MP: American Art Under the New Deal: Murals, in *Art in Australia*, 3rd Series, no. 69 (November).
MP: Running round the Americas, in *Home* 18, no. 11 (November).

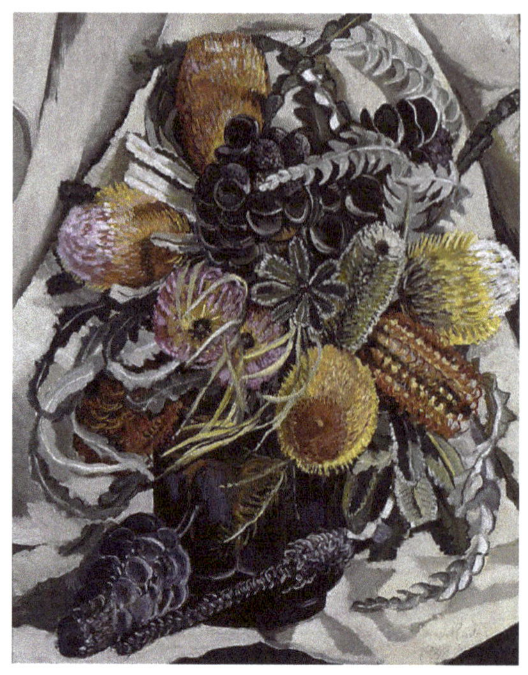

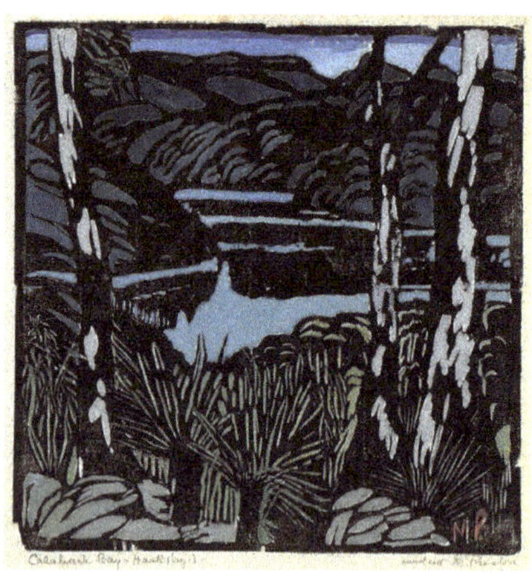

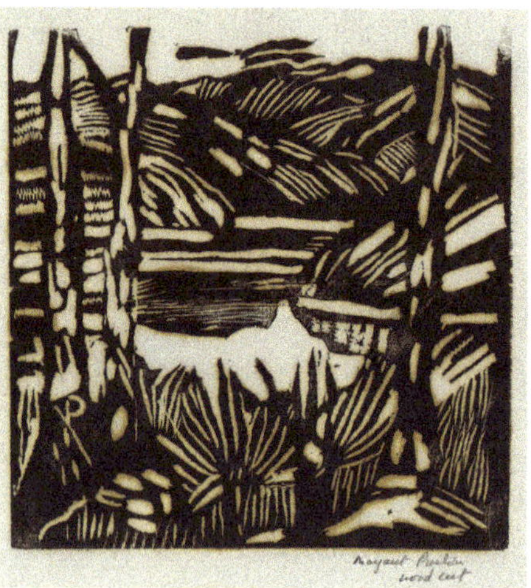

Banksia, 1938, oil on canvas. Art Gallery of New South Wales.
Cowan Creek, from Berowra, c. 1939, woodblock, Art Gallery of New South Wales.
Calabash Bay, Berowra, 1939, woodblock, National Gallery of Australia.

1938 - Berowra: Electricity activated in the town.
Sydney, 27 January to 25 April, *150 Years of Australian Art*, Art Gallery of NSW.
Sydney 18 to 31 March, *Group Exhibition*, Grosvenor Galleries.
Sydney, 8 to 29 April, *Australian Academy of Art, First Exhibition*, Education Department's Art Gallery.
MP attended Ms Frances Street's exhibition of posters in Sydney, noting that "a love of colour was characteristic of deeper mental development."
MP: Five Lectures Given in the National Art Gallery of NSW, in *Art in Australia*, 3rd Series, no. 72 (August), with the lectures beginning on August 1.
Sydney, 3 to 30 September, *Society of Artists, Annual Exhibition*, Education Department's Art Gallery.
MP in London studying at the London School of Decoration.
Berowra Post Office is fully operational on 12 September.
Sydney, *(Paintings for Australian Pavilion, New York World Fair)*, Art Gallery of NSW.

1939 - Melbourne, 5 April to 3 May, *Australian Academy of Art, Second Exhibition,* National Gallery of Victoria.
Adelaide, 17 May to 7 June, *Australian Academy of Art, Second Exhibition,* Art Gallery of South Australia.
New York, 30 April to ?, *Australian Pavilion, New York World Fair.*
Berowra Waters women make camouflage nets.
Sydney, 4 to 25 August, *Society of Artists, Annual Exhibition*, Education Department's Art Gallery.
Berowra: Prestons sell their house, 'The Springs' and move to 14 Thompson Street, Mosman producing prints like Cowan Creek, from Berowra.
Sydney, 14 September to 4 October, *Society of Arts and Crafts of NSW,* Education Department's Art Gallery.
San Francisco, October to?, *Australian Pavilion, Golden Gate Exposition.*
Wellington, 1939, *Australian Pavilion, New Zealand Centenary Exhibition.*
MP: Crafts that Aid, in *Art in Australia*, 3rd Series, no. 77 (November).

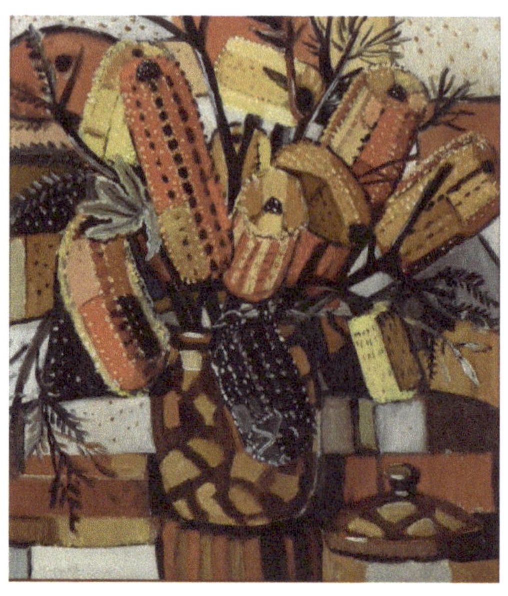

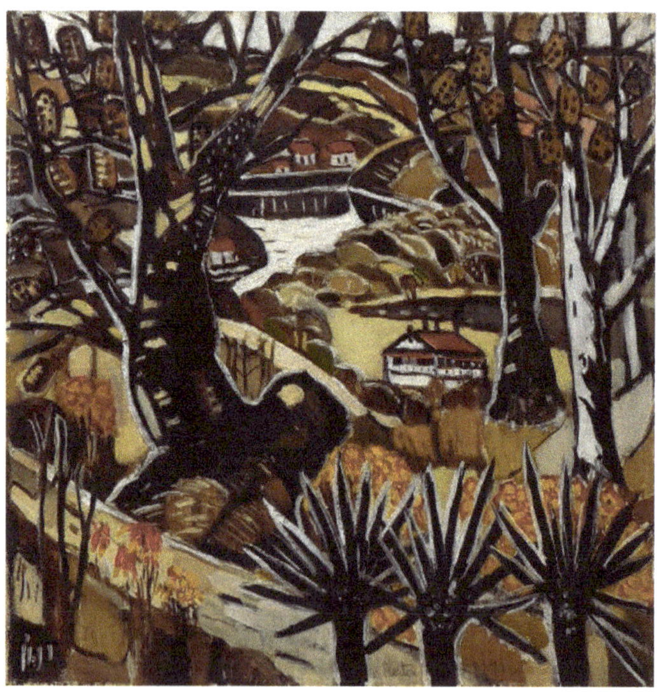

The Brown Pot, 1940, oil on canvas. Art Gallery of New South Wales.
I Lived At Berowra, 1941, oil on canvas. Art Gallery of New South Wales.

1940 - Sydney, March 30 to April 18, *Australian Academy of Art, Third Exhibition*, Education Department's Art Gallery.

Sydney 6 to 25 September, *Society of Artists, Annual Exhibition*, Education Department's Art Gallery.

MP: Painting in Arnhem Land, in *Art in Australia*, 3rd Series, no. 81 (November).

1941 - MP: Australia Ahoy, in *Australian National Journal*, 2, no. 2 (January).

MP: 'O' is for Orange, in *Australian National Journal*, 2, no. 4 (March).

Melbourne 6 April – 16 May, *Australian Academy of Art, 4th Annual Exhibition*, Athenaeum Gallery.

MP: New Developments in Australian Art, in *Australian National Journal*, 2, no. 6 (May).

MP: Newcastle of Australia, in *Australian National Journal*, 2, no. 6 (May).

MP: Aboriginal Art, in *Art in Australia*, 4th Series, no.2 (June).

MP: Tallong Trot, in *Australian National Journal*, 2, no. 8 (July).

Sydney, 11 to 22 August, *Australian Aboriginal Art and its Application*, David Jones Auditorium.

Sydney 5 to 25 September, *Society of Artists, Annual Exhibition*, Education Department's Art Gallery; AGNSW purchased I Lived at Berowra.

MP: Aboriginal Art of Australia, in *Catalogue of Art in Australia 1788-1941* (Ure Smith).

MP: Some Aspects of Painting in Australia, in *Cultural Cross Section* (Jindywarabak).

USA and Canada, 2 October to ?, *Art of Australia Exhibition 1788-1941*, Fine Art Museum, Yale University and touring from there.

Berowra, major bushfire at Berowra Waters, High Street areas.

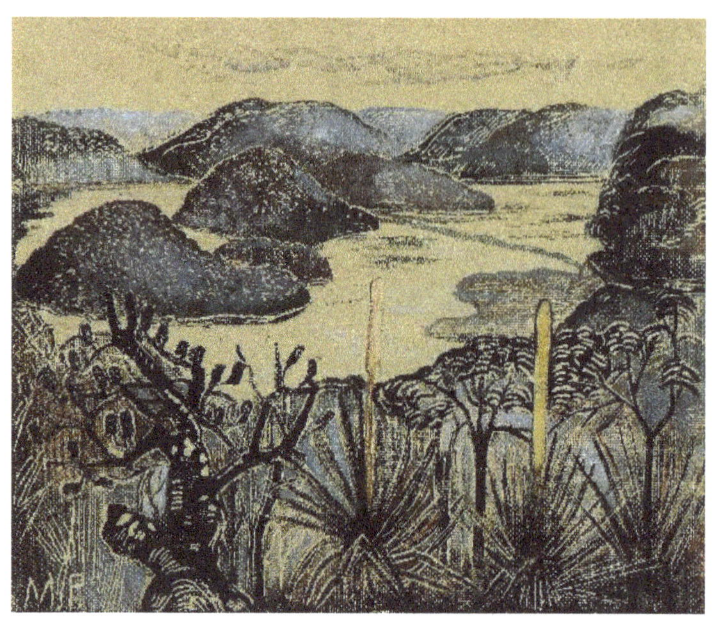

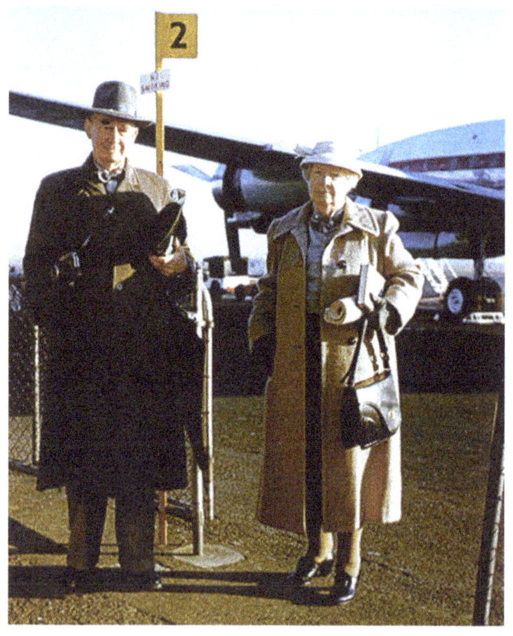

Hawkesbury River, 1945, Monotype. Private Collection.
William and Margaret Preston, 1954.

1942 - MP: By Gannet! Here's Boydtown, in *Australian National Journal* 3, no. 3 (February).

Sydney, 25 February to 9 March, *A Collection of Prints*, Macquarie Galleries.

Sydney 19 March to 16 April, *Margaret Preston and William Dobell Loan Exhibition*, Art Gallery of NSW.

1945 - Prestons move into the Hotel Mosman, where they reside for 11 years.

1947 - *Margaret Preston's Monotypes* published by Ure Smith.

1956 - Prestons move to 22 Killarney Street, Mosman.

1958 - MP delivers a final lecture 'Aboriginal paintings – Arnhem Land' at the Art Gallery of New South Wales.

Prestons make a final overseas trip to India from September to December.

1963 - Margaret Preston died at Mosman on 28 May.

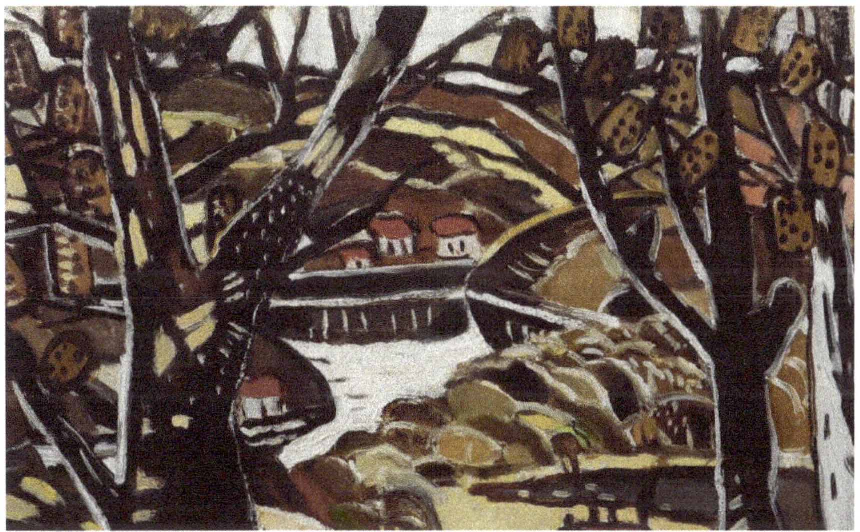

I lived at Berowra, 1941 (detail). Oil on Canvas. Art Gallery of New South Wales.

Notes

In 1933 newspaper article on Preston, art critic, Howard Ashton noted in regard to the artist's work that one could even "tell what flowers are at my feet". See Butler, R 2005, *The Prints of Margaret Preston: A Catalogue Raisonne*, National Gallery of Australia, Canberra, p. 25. A small section of this essay has been extracted from an article by the author that appeared in the September 2005 issue of *Art & Australia.*

The Preston rugs were first revealed to the public in late June, 2005: Moses, A 2005, 'The rugs that have the art experts floored', *Sydney Morning Herald*, 29 June, p. 9.

Interviews were undertaken by the author with a number of Berowra locals: the late Bill Foster, the late Peter Huett, the late Pam Gartung, Rhonda Coleman, Shirley Collins, Robyn Ellison and Garry Smith.

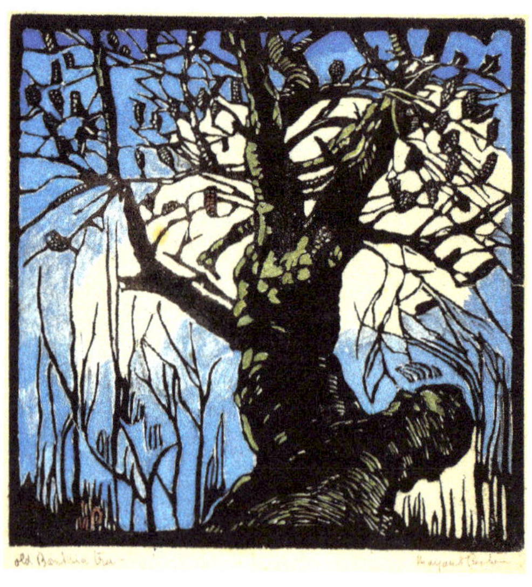

The Banksia Tree, hand-coloured woodcut, 1939.
National Gallery of Australia.

End Notes

1 *A Guide to Berowra Valley Regional Park* 2001, Friends of Berowra Valley Regional Park, Sydney.
2 Rickard, A 1910, 'Beautiful Berowra', extract from *The Sydney Morning Herald*, 13 December 1910, p. 11.
3 1932, pers. comm. to John Young, 23 July. Letters to John Young sourced from, Macquarie Galleries archive, Art Gallery of New South Wales, Research Library, Sydney.
4 1932, pers. comm. To John Young 17 November. As above.
5 'The World and His Wife', *Sunday Times* (Sydney, NSW:1895-1930), Sunday 20 December 1914, p.5.
6 'Tramped 150 Miles for "The Referee"', *Referee* (Sydney), Wednesday 8 September 1926, p. 16.
7 'An Air of Space...Even the Small Cottage Need Not Be Cramped', *Sydney Morning Herald*, Friday 10 November 1933, p. 4.
8 *The Bulletin*, Vol.54. 22 November 1933.
9 Ibid.
10 Nora Cooper, 1937, 'Margaret Preston at home', *The Australian Home Beautiful*, 15. No. 2, 1 February, pp. 28–52.
11 'Women Artists', *Sydney Morning Herald,* Wednesday 13 September 1933, p. 5.
12 1933, pers. comm. to John Young, 10 May. Letters to John Young sourced from Macquarie Galleries archive, Art Gallery of New South Wales, Research Library, Sydney.
13 Op. cit. no. 10. p.52.
14 Op. cit. no. 10. p.52.
15 1933, pers. comm. to John Young, 22 May. Letters to John Young sourced from Macquarie Galleries archive, Art Gallery of New South Wales, Research Library, Sydney.

16 Arthur Rickard, 'Beautiful Berowra', extract from the *Sydney Morning Herald*, 13 December 1910, p. 13.

17 The pump is indicated is on a site plan of the property and its amenities at the time of its purchase by the Smith family shortly after the Prestons sold the property. Courtesy of Roger Butler

18 Op. cit. no. 10. P.52.

19 Op. cit. no. 10. P.52.

20 Ian North, 1980, 'Margaret Preston, Model of an Era', *The Art of Margaret Preston*, Art Gallery of South Australia, note 25, p. 14.

21 'Tea on the lawn', *The Sun* (Sydney, NSW: 1910-1954) Sunday 27 February 1938.

22 Myra Payne 1973, pers. comm. to Mick Joffe, 26 Dec.

23 Peter Huett, 2005 pers. comm. to author, 10 June.

24 'Advertising', the *Sydney Morning Herald*, Saturday 29 December 1923, p. 16.

25 Shirley Collins, 2005, pers. comm. to author, 27 April.

26 Ibid.

27 Myra Payne 1973, pers. comm. to Mick Joffe, 26 December.

28 'The World and His Wife', *Sunday Times* (Sydney, NSW) Sunday 20 December 1914, p. 5.

29 'Art Exhibitions: Contemporary Painters' *Sydney Morning Herald,* Thursday 29 November 1928, p. 15.

30 Robyn Ellison, 2005, pers. comm. to author.

31 Ibid.

32 Rhonda Coleman, 2005, pers. comm. to author 8 February.

33 Ibid.

34 Myra Payne, 1973, pers. comm. to Mick Joffe, 26 December.

35 Rhonda Coleman, 2005, pers. comm. to author, 8 February.

36 Mick Joffe, *Yarns & Photos Beautiful Old Berowra & Hornsby to the Hawkesbury*, 1992, Sandstone Press, p.127.

37 Bill Foster, 2005, pers. comm. to author, 10 June.

38 Letter to John Young October 1934

39 'This Week's Prizewinners', *Australian Women's Weekly*, Saturday 15 January 1938, p. 6.
40 Margaret Preston, 'The Indigenous Art of Australia', *Art in Australia,* 1925, Sydney, 3rd series, no. 11, March, p. 49.
41 Margaret Preston, 'The Indigenous Art of Australia', *Art in Australia,* 1925, Sydney, 3rd series, no. 11, March, p. 51.
42 1933, pers. comm. to John Young, 22 May. Letters to John Young sourced from Macquarie Galleries archive, Art Gallery of New South Wales, Research Library, Sydney.
43 Roy de Maistre created a rug design that was never produced. The drawing is held in the National Gallery of Australia, Canberra Collection.
44 Mark Davis, 2005, pers. comm. to author.
45 Humphrey McQueen, 'An Enemy of the Dull', *Hemisphere,* 1976, Vol 20, No. 8, August pp. 34–40.
46 Jennifer Issacs, *The Gentle Arts: 200 Years of Australian Women's Domestic and Decorative Arts,* 1987, Lansdowne Press, Sydney.
47 John McPhee, 'Helen Ogilvie' in Joan Kerr (ed), *Heritage: The National Women's Art Book*, Craftsman House, Sydney, 1995, p. 251.
48 Beth Hatton, 'Handmade, Underfoot', in S. Carlin (ed) *Floorcoverings in Australia 1800–1950*, Historic Houses Trust of NSW, Sydney, 1997, p25
49 Margaret Preston, 'The Indigenous Art of Australia', *Art in Australia,* 1925, 3rd Series, no. 11.
50 'Gum Blossoms Packed in Ice for Artist', *Daily Telegraph* (Sydney, NSW: 1931–1954) Saturday 27 February 1937, p. 11.
51 Ibid.
52 Ibid.
53 Ibid.
54 Op. cit. no. 7.
55 Letter to John Young, Sunday 1935.

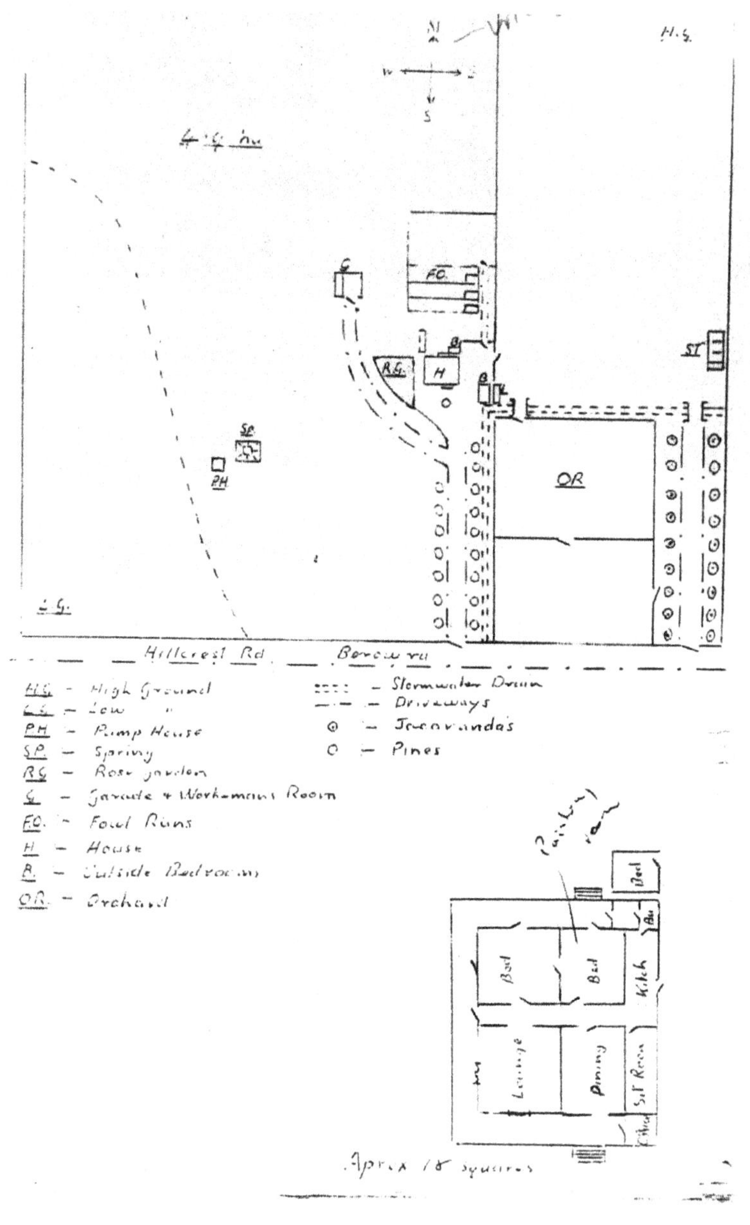

Original plan of Preston's 'The Springs' property on Hillcrest Road, Berowra.

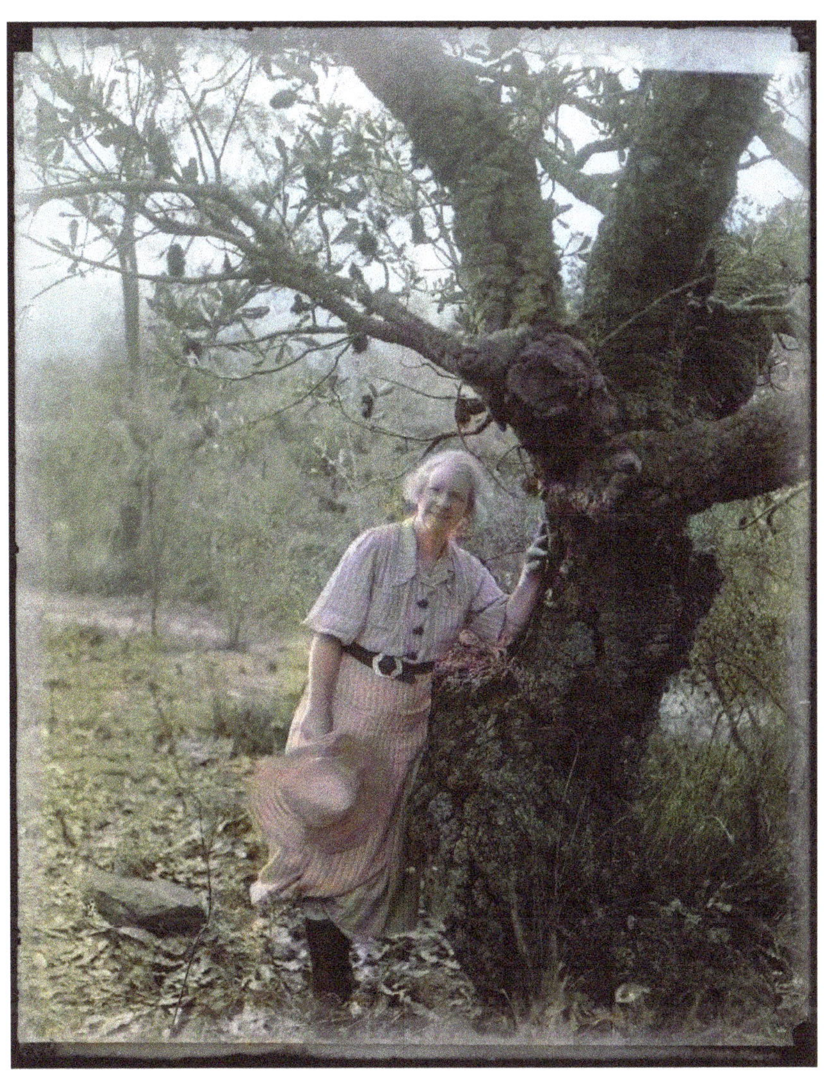

Harold Cazneaux's portrait of Margaret Preston with her favourite banksia on The Springs property, 1936.

Also by Margaret Preston

SELECTED WRITINGS by Margaret Preston - Compiled by Elizabeth Butel, offering over 30 of Preston's articles, including her own memoirs, ideas on craft and design, and her essays on indigenous art in Australia.
117 pages, ISBN 978-1-923024-67-0

APHORISMS by Margaret Preston - First published in Preston's *Recent Paintings* in 1929, these are Preston's own words: "A lemon can be an inspiration, as well as a fruit."
40 pages, ISBN 978-0-925416-76-3

MONOTYPES - First published in a limited edition in 1948, this is available as an ebook only.
66 pages, ISBN 978-1-925706-09-3

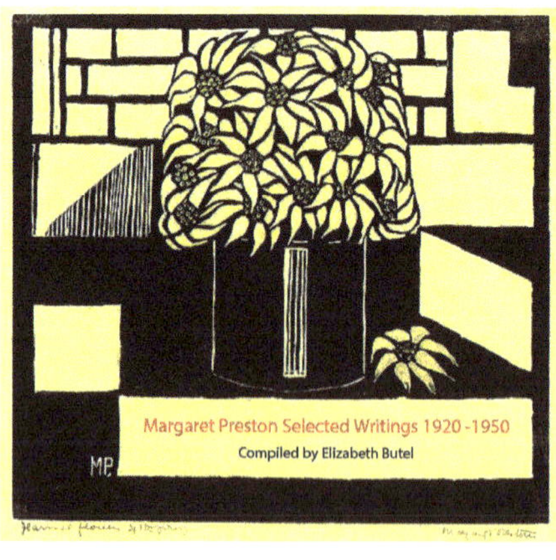

APHORISMS by
MARGARET
PRESTON

www.ingramcontent.com/pod-product-compliance
Lightning Source LLC
LaVergne TN
LVHW052348100826
845147LV00012B/785

* 9 7 8 1 9 2 3 2 0 5 8 7 1 *